To Darlene:

There is power in the dream... never give upon yours!

Love
Janet.

MindWealth™

MindWealth™

Turning Knowledge into Assets

Janet K. Slemko, MA/ABS

BookPartners
Wilsonville, Oregon

MindWealth™ is a registered trademark of Janet Slemko.

BookPartners, Inc.
P. O. Box 922
Wilsonville, Oregon 97071

To those who dare to act on their dreams.

Contents

Part I. Self-Knowledge: Reclaim Individual Power

Part II. Unleash Team Knowledge

Part III. Achieve Organization Synergy

Acknowledgments

My special thanks to:

- Patricia Ahnn Axten for your love and support, and for our walks and discussions that opened up a whole new world for me.

- Linda Raven for always being there with insights, love, and encouragement to continue the process.

- Leslie Johnson, Bob Fuller, and Mary Pat Barry for reading and strengthening the manuscript.

- Kathleen Ennis for the book layout and for hanging in with me through all the rewrites.

- My family and friends whose support and belief in me makes my work possible.

Introduction

At the dawn of a new millennium—a time of transitions and new opportunities—unleashing the hidden assets within ourselves and within our organizations has never been more important. In today's global markets, technology reshapes our lives, globalization continually changes the rules of competition, and the information age alters the ways in which we interact. These changes have redefined the underlying economic structure. Experience no longer guarantees success and economic power has shifted from labor-intensive production to a fast-paced, knowledge-based world where knowledge and information are more valuable than land, labor, or equipment.

In today's knowledge economy, the future value of a company will be created through the development of strategic assets that establish new innovative capabilities. Wealth is a product of intellectual assets that provide a competitive advantage. Economic growth is dependent upon development and transfer of the organization's collective knowledge into new value-added services and products.

In this new economy, knowledge is more important than information. Knowledge is the ability to put information into use by being aware of and understanding the surrounding context that gives the information meaning. It is this understanding that makes the information useful as knowledge that can be practically applied.

Knowledge is the primary ingredient in everything we buy, do, or sell, and is embedded in the social fabric of an organization's relationships, processes, and capabilities. In each organization, a specific core of knowledge determines how the business operates—its mission, values, procedures, processes, and decision-making. This core of knowledge sets the foundation for the organization's ability to be flexible and adaptable in a changing environment. In order to convert an organization's know-how (the sum total of its knowledge, skills, experiences, insights, and lessons) into a competitive advantage, a climate must be established where tacit knowledge (knowledge contained within an individual's experience) is understood and shared (thereby becoming explicit knowledge) to generate new perspectives and optimize performance.

To survive — and thrive — in the marketplace requires a radically different approach to management and leadership. Success depends on creating new skills, new kinds of organizations and new ways to manage. The key skills are mental rather than physical. Individual success is based on the ability to change personally and to adapt to a changing world and to put ideas, concepts, and information to work in a new way.

In order to be competitive in this knowledge era, what changes will be required? What must an organization do to effectively utilize its collective knowledge, and what will businesses need to do differently? As I pondered these questions, I reflected back on my twenty-seven-year career as a teacher, manager, and consultant in public and private organizations. During this time, I coached individuals in developing their leadership skills, and I worked with corporations to establish their key values and helped them create and implement total quality, re-engineering and restructuring programs. Although these processes focused a lot of attention on change, I noticed that very little lasting change resulted. I began to wonder: What creates change? What hinders or prevents lasting change?

The Nature of Change

I realized that, as individuals, we grapple with two types of change — change that we initiate ourselves and change that is imposed upon us from the outside. When I observed that externally motivated change often elicited defensive responses and rarely achieved lasting results, I concluded that true, lasting change must begin inside — and be initiated by the individual. It quickly became apparent that organizational change is impossible unless the individuals within the organization genuinely embrace the change. Real change is an internal process that begins within each individual and works its way out into the organization moment by moment.

The Key Is Self-Knowledge

Knowledge is dynamic, fluid, and ever-changing. What the knower knows is shaped by the level of his understanding, thinking, and reasoning processes. For new knowledge and information to have meaning, we must translate it into our own frames of references. To each interaction or situation, we bring a complex set of skills, behaviors, mental processes, and past experiences that establish the boundaries of the event. Lasting change occurs only when we gain self-knowledge of our experiences and understand how our thoughts, beliefs, and values guide our decisions and behaviors.

Self-knowledge is the process of focusing our attention inwardly in order to examine the inner dimension of our experiences and to become aware of our thoughts and perceptions. Our ability to observe our own participation in an event allows us to consciously choose new behaviors and actions and to apply these to new situations. The level of knowledge gained is determined by our openness and willingness to explore new avenues.

My Journey

My desire to understand how the process of change works on an organizational level led me on a personal journey to discover the power of change within myself. The road to understanding was a winding path of certainty, uncertainty, and a lot of questions, but each step moved me to a new level of awareness about myself and how I can implement change in my life. I finally realized that internal change comes through a change in consciousness.

Let's take the mystique out of the word "consciousness." Human consciousness is simply the combination of thoughts, attitudes, beliefs, and sensitivities (the capacity to respond to stimulation) that characterizes each individual. In the context in which we're speaking, "changing our consciousness" is simply the result of choosing a new or different set of thoughts, beliefs, attitudes, and responses. When we finally understand that we can control our consciousness moment by moment, we unlock the power of change within ourselves.

As I became more aware of my own consciousness, I noticed how my thoughts could shift quickly from confidence to fear—from feeling centered and balanced to feeling anxious and unsettled. I noticed the words I used and the focus of my conversations. I became aware of my reactions and how easily my thoughts would shift. I examined the reactions of others and how those reactions affected me. I realized that I was merely reacting to the circumstances around me rather than engaging each moment with an active, purposeful mind. And I discovered that I often reacted based on past experience and prior conditioning rather than by deliberate, conscious choice. I started to understand that affirmations conditioned my thoughts, but the focus of my thoughts from moment to moment created the direction of my day. I decided to catch myself reacting and to refocus my thoughts whenever necessary.

Discovering My Power

At first I wasn't aware of my thoughts, but I began to notice my reactions during meetings, conversations, and other situations. When I caught myself in a reaction, I struggled to adjust my thoughts to align them more closely with my desires and purpose for that situation. Over time, with patience and persistence, I started to become aware of my thoughts as they were occurring. To heighten my awareness, I asked questions like, "What is happening right now? What am I thinking or feeling in this moment? What is this situation telling me about myself? What can I learn from this? What do I want to experience right now?"

The more I observed my thoughts and reactions, the more I felt empowered and in control of my life. Each situation and interaction became a learning laboratory—a place to explore, observe and understand. I noticed how I felt as I was listening to the news or reading a report or talking to someone. I looked at how my thinking was affected by other people's expectations, opinions and beliefs, and I learned that I needed to stand guard at the doorway of my mind in order to create the life I desired.

I became aware that many of the messages I received were based on fear and limitation. For example, I was fascinated by the reaction of my colleagues and friends when I told them I was writing a book. Instead of responding with excitement and interest, they usually asked me a limiting question based on fear: "Do you have a publisher?" It was as if there was no purpose in writing the book unless I had external validation (in the form of a signed publishing contract) and assurance that everything was guaranteed and worked out in advance.

Each reaction and situation provided food for thought as I reflected on the decisions and choices I had made in my life that were based on fear and insecurity. This led me to think about the foundation for many organizational changes and decisions. As I looked back on the total quality, re-engineering and restructuring processes I had assisted in, I asked the question, "What would happen if organizational energy shifted from an external focus to concentrate on unlocking the power within each individual?"

I am convinced that the pathway to creating a work environment that is not only successful and profitable, but also exciting, exhilarating and fulfilling, lies in creating a shift from externally imposed change to internally motivated and activated change. It is only through a change in consciousness—that is, a change in our beliefs, attitudes, and sensitivities—that lasting change can be accomplished. As long as organizations implement purely external changes—changes that fail to touch individuals at the level of consciousness—those changes will not last. On the other hand, when individuals begin to experience their true potential and unleash their internal powers of commitment, creativity, learning and leverage, organizations will naturally and inevitably be transformed in the process.

Create What You Want

Throughout *MindWealth,* I talk about "creating what you want." This catch phrase is my way of saying "making decisions that are consistent with your values, goals, beliefs, and desires."

MindWealth is built on the following foundation:

- Each of us already has the "power within" to solve any challenges we face.

- Power is released through our thoughts, choices, and actions.

- The future unfolds and is shaped moment by moment.

- Every moment, every situation and every change is a new opportunity to control our own destiny.

- Every asset within the individual is available to the team or the organization to the extent that individual energy is unlocked and utilized.

Seize the Moment

Right now—this very moment—you have a decision to make that will profoundly affect your life and the future of your organization. Will you choose to tap into the immense wealth of knowledge, creativity and positive energy that lies hidden inside of you and your company, or will you decide to leave these valuable resources untouched and unexamined and simply get back to work?

As an individual, will you choose to continue to react to the world around you based on past experience and prior conditioning, or will you recognize that you have control over your own consciousness—your thoughts, beliefs, attitudes and responses—and dare to make a difference, starting right now?

The choice is yours, and the decision you make—or don't make—will profoundly affect the future of your business and your life.

*A journey of a thousand miles
begins with a footstep.*

—Tao Te Ching

Part I

Self-Knowledge: Reclaim Individual Power

*A state of mind is the one and only thing
over which a person has complete,
unchallenging right of control.*

—Napoleon Hill

*We become what we are
by the choices we make.*

—Marva Collins

Chapter 1

Unleash the Power

The Power Within

Unlocking your personal energy occurs in the present moment. Change happens moment by moment when we consciously choose to see a situation differently and choose a different response. Tapping into the power within ourselves is a process of harnessing the potential of three key currents of energy: the power of thought, the power of choice, and the power of action.

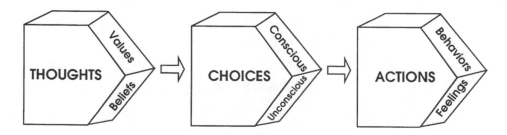

Each moment provides a new opportunity to choose how we will perceive our experiences. In any situation, we have the choice to simply react according to past experience and prior conditioning, or we can decide to adapt our perception and consciously choose a response. For example, we can reply to a comment from a coworker by getting angry, by laughing, by remaining detached, by responding logically, or any number of other responses. The choice we make will change our experience of that moment and will influence our coworker accordingly. Thus, by changing ourselves we influence the world around us in a direction consistent with our internal desires.

What we think, feel, or imagine influences our experiences. Our thoughts are pictures of reality that we hold in our minds. These pictures create boundaries and limits. They define how we see ourselves and what we believe we can or cannot do. The orientation of our thoughts in the present moment is determined by our values (what we value as important) and our beliefs (what we hold to be true). We bring assumptions created through past experiences into the present moment to form conscious or unconscious choices. These choices determine our actions—our behaviors (what we do and how we do it)—or our feelings (emotional responses) about the situation. Self-awareness or self-knowledge allows us to consciously choose to disengage the "automatic pilot" (our unconscious responses) and choose a new direction by expanding our limiting beliefs, responding from a higher viewpoint, or interrupting disempowering patterns.

Thoughts create a focus and this focus establishes a direction for our actions. For example, are we focused on success or focused on failure? When we look for what is good in a situation or what we can learn from it, a pattern of thought is created to support our success. When we look at what is wrong or not working, we create thoughts of anxiety and worry.

These patterns of thoughts are created by our beliefs. Thus, what we believe will affect the outcomes we achieve. For example, if we believe something will be hard to do, often it will be. When we awaken to the reality that our lives are unfolding moment by moment, we can consciously guide our thoughts, choose our responses, and direct our actions.

Access the Power

A few years ago, Jan Carlzon, the dynamic president and CEO of Scandinavian Airlines (SAS), described each customer interaction as a "moment of truth." He explained that each moment of truth created how the customer would perceive SAS in the future. Carlzon recognized that each moment was an opportunity for his employees to feel needed and to make a difference in the direction and success of the company. He saw that his business consisted of thousands of moments of truth—each one as important as the next.

We all have our own moments of truth—whether it's on the job, at home with our families, or in social interactions. Each moment is unique. Each moment is an opportunity to access our personal power by accepting the situation as it is, experiencing the moment fully, and sensing the energies around us.

Acknowledge the Situation

Unlocking the power of the moment is the process of identifying what is happening and accepting the situation the way it is. When we acknowledge the situation, we take responsibility for the part we play in creating it—recognizing our strengths and weaknesses and becoming aware of our thoughts, feelings, and choices.

Experience the Moment

Moment-by-moment awareness means focusing our attention on where we are right now, without fear or worry about the future or the past. If we walk into a room thinking about someone or worrying about paying the bills, we are not consciously focused in the present. The more in touch we are with the present, the more we can make conscious choices to respond in ways that are consistent with our values, goals, beliefs, and desires.

Living in the present doesn't mean giving up on our dreams, aspirations, or hopes, but it does mean giving up on our concerns about the past or the future. To live in the present is to see each moment as an opportunity to start fresh—without old thoughts and distorted attitudes. It's having a childlike excitement and anticipation of what will happen next.

Reducing self-interference. To fully open to the experience requires a willingness to get out of the way. Our capacity to perform effectively is in direct proportion to the stillness of our minds. By quieting our minds, and letting go of distracting thoughts, we can experience each moment more fully.

Throughout the day, when my thoughts gravitate to worries, I take a moment to quiet my mind. I close my eyes and take three deep breaths to release the negative energy. I then imagine, in my mind's eye, a hot-air balloon. I insert each anxious thought into the balloon and release it skyward. As I visualize the colorful canopy moving up, up, and away, I take another deep breath and release any residual tension.

Self-discovery. The second prerequisite for living in the moment is the willingness to accept ambiguity and explore new behaviors. Letting go of old patterns to make room for new ones means setting aside what we think we know and releasing our stranglehold on the past. Give yourself a gift—allow yourself to be where you are. Give yourself permission to allow each moment to unfold exactly as it is and allow yourself to be exactly as you are. Create an attitude of curiosity. Ask, "What can I learn from this?"

In order to create a receptive attitude, I remind myself before business meetings that I want to fully experience each moment. I remind myself that I am an explorer of the moment and that each moment has something of value to teach me.

Focused attention. Every experience is a learning opportunity. Capturing the power of the present moment means to see a situation clearly and choose a different response or action. This awareness can help us in many different ways if we are open to observing how we are feeling as well as how others are responding to us.

For example, I remember one of the first times I worked in the telecommunications industry. I met with two network planners from a large telephone company that was modernizing its network. Our purpose was to explore the impact of technological changes on the workforce and to discuss how best to implement the new technology and changes. I did not have a technical background and I soon became aware that I lacked the necessary expertise to be effective in the discussions. As I tuned into my sense of uneasiness, I realized that I needed to take decisive action. I told the planners that if I could take the technical manuals back to my hotel and study them overnight, I could be more effective in analyzing the impacts. I spent my evening in intensive study, and next day I was able to hold my own in the discussion. This resulted in the two companies developing a long-term relationship of sharing information.

Each situation is an opportunity to increase our awareness of our own internal strengths and weaknesses, and to use that awareness to learn and grow. Awareness doesn't change our behavior—it only allows us to make a choice to do something different. Here are some suggestions to help you awaken yourself to the experience of the moment:

- Develop daily reminders to pull your attention back to the present. I developed a motto—"Today's Actions Create Tomorrow's Future"—which I posted on my office wall above my desk. When I noticed my thoughts moving to worries about the past or future, I used my motto as an affirmation to pull myself back into the present.

- Take time each day to observe your surroundings. Observe your office, home or neighborhood and notice what catches your attention. Observe what changes over time. When I drive home along a familiar route, I ask myself, "Am I in the present moment? What do I notice right now?" I'm continually amazed at my discovery of the changes—road improvements, new buildings, new trees.

- Ask questions during the moment to observe your thoughts and reactions. I often ask myself, "What am I thinking or feeling right now? What would I like to feel?" These questions not only allow me to observe my thoughts and reactions, but they shift my internal energy toward creating the life I want.

- Review an event, or the day, and notice the focus of your attention. I often take a minute to close my eyes and think about a situation and observe where my thoughts lead. Then I review the situation and see it as I would like it to be in the future.

- Engage in a conversation with someone and notice the words that you use. Paying attention to what I say helps me become aware of habitual feelings that I would like to change.

- Stimulate your thinking by asking questions. Ask yourself, "How is my life different today than one year ago?" This question reminds me that I'm always growing and learning and that nothing stays the same. During challenging times, this question helps me to realize that "this too shall pass," and it changes my focus to one of gratitude for all that I have in my life.

You can perform these centering activities in a few minutes. When I first decided to concentrate on becoming more present in the moment, I resisted steps like the ones I'm suggesting because I told myself I was too busy. With all the meetings I attended in the course of a day, I didn't think I would be able to stop and focus. But then I realized that my thoughts were occurring during the meeting regardless of what was being said or done. So, I started to experiment with ways of observing my thoughts. I found that I became more attuned to everything that was happening around me. As a result, I became more effective in the meetings.

Sense the Energy

We all make decisions based on the energy we sense, and we are constantly sensing energy whether we are consciously aware of it or not. We are like TV satellites receiving many different, simultaneous messages. What we respond to depends on where we focus our attention. For example, when we meet someone for the first time, we instantly decide whether or not we like that person. Or when we walk into a room where two people are having an angry discussion, we immediately feel the tension.

Awareness. By focusing our attention, we increase our awareness of the present moment. This process operates like the zoom lens on a camera. We possess a number of different settings which allow us to zoom in or zoom out of a situation. At any moment, we can choose to adjust our awareness lenses and move to a sharper level of focus.

The following four focus levels allow us to gain clarity and understanding of our surroundings.

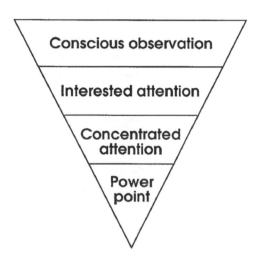

Conscious observation is noticing what is going on while it's going on. When we consciously observe our surroundings, we notice the sights, sounds, feelings, and thoughts that create our present experience. What are you thinking, seeing, feeling right now?

Interested attention is awareness driven by curiosity or the desire to know more about something. Ask yourself, "What can I learn from this experience?"

Concentrated attention is focusing our minds deliberately, like a laser beam, on one specific spot or area. The purpose of concentrated attention is to gain specific details about a particular area.

Power point is the ability to be totally immersed or absorbed in the moment without thinking about the past or the future.

Each subsequently deeper level increases our capability to know our surroundings. By effectively and quickly moving between levels, we can gather information about the energy around us. This information enables us to change our responses to the events we are experiencing, and thereby increases our ability to respond in ways that are consistent with our values.

Awareness skills are like any other skills. They are developed over time through practice and use. Every situation is an opportunity to develop our skills. Learn to observe others as well as yourself. Start wherever your attention takes you.

Whenever I walk into a room, I focus my attention and observe what is going on. Where are people sitting? Who is talking to whom? Is conversation light and easygoing or intense business talk? What is the tone or mood? What happens when I walk in? Does anything change?

After a few moments, I focus on my own energy. I become aware of my thoughts, feelings and physiological responses. I notice the effect others have on my emotions and I pay attention to sudden shifts in energy. If I am paying attention, every interaction tells me something about myself. The more aware I am, the less outside influences can affect me.

The key to effective awareness is detached observation, a process of simply noticing what is occurring without expectation or judgment. It means becoming aware of what is happening without reacting to it. Detached observation requires a letting go of likes and dislikes as well as any preconceived ideas of what should be occurring. It is a process of simply acknowledging what is happening—"I'm thinking about tomorrow's meeting," or "There seems to be a lot of concern about this issue." Detachment is like taking a step back to watch the moment without trying to change anything. This provides an opportunity to assess the circumstances from a higher viewpoint—to see the patterns of activity and energy that keep the situation as it is. This new perspective enables us to identify what actions we need to take to align with our purpose.

When I surrender into the moment, I can experience wholeness. I can experience my thoughts, feelings and fears completely. This acknowledgment frees me to see the situation differently and opens me to new possibilities. By letting go of preconceived ideas, I can see each situation as non-permanent and thereby shift my focus to create the experience I want.

Your life is your work of art.

—Shakti Gawain

The more you depend on forces outside yourself,
the more you are dominated by them.

—Harold Sherman

True life is lived when tiny changes occur.

—Leo Tolstoy

Chapter 2

Start Where You Are

Change Comes From Within

Our perceptions and experiences in each moment are a reflection of our thoughts, beliefs and attitudes about the world around us. We experience and respond to our environment through our five senses—sight, sound, touch, taste and smell—but we perceive things not necessarily as they are objectively, but as they appear through the filter of our consciousness. Our representations of reality determine how we behave and give meaning to our behavior.

The mind stores all our thoughts and feelings and accepts the emotions, fears and limitations that we teach it. The subconscious mind is like a large map on which our life experiences are recorded. Focusing our attention in the present moment is like shining a beam of light on a small section of a darkened map. As we change our focus, we illuminate different areas of our maps. When we choose to actively control our consciousness, we make a deliberate decision to shine the light on a specific part of our internal map. Wherever we shine the light determines what we see and how we see it.

Every belief, attitude and response that has taken shape in our lives began as a thought. When we examine everything we have created in our lives—good or bad—we are looking at a snapshot of our thoughts and feelings. In order to change the world around us, we must alter our perspective and shift our response. The choices we make create the ways in which we experience reality. We have the power and the freedom to create and shape our consciousness and to fulfill our dreams.

The first step toward change is to recognize that where we are today is a result of past choices. Life is a series of choices. Each thought or feeling results from a conscious or unconscious decision. Every moment is a new opportunity to choose our consciousness: either by deliberately controlling our thoughts, beliefs, and responses, or by defaulting to the inertia of past experiences or prior conditioning. Either option is open to us every moment, and in every moment we decide—either consciously or not—how we will respond or act.

One choice leads to another—one moment at a time—and change occurs one decision at a time. Each shift in our perspective creates a ripple effect that leads to another shift.

When I find myself upset, frustrated or angry, I ask myself, "What am I choosing to feel right now? How would I like to feel?" By consciously and intentionally posing the questions, I acknowledge my responsibility for my feelings and attitudes in the present moment and I take deliberate control of my responses and actions.

When we choose our responses instead of reacting from past experience, we shift the locus of control from the unconscious to the conscious. Now, instead of acting like victims, we gain control of our lives, which enables us to create the outcomes that we desire. This shift requires a willingness to change—a willingness to take responsibility for acting differently.

A few years ago, I made a decision to leave a group of colleagues and start on a new path. That night, during a conversation with a friend, I told him I was feeling lonely and uncertain. My friend, reminding me that every thought and feeling is a choice, asked, "How long do you want to feel this way?" I immediately laughed and responded in a mock-indignant voice, "At least few more minutes!" We both enjoyed a good laugh, but his question was the catalyst that helped me to shift my thoughts and feelings back under conscious control. Soon, I was talking about the future and the dreams that had led me to the decision I had made.

Identify What You Want

When we decide to make a change or achieve a new goal, we must clearly focus our minds on the objective by being specific about what we want, and intending to have it. Clear intention directs our thoughts and focuses our energy—like a laser beam—toward achieving our dreams. This focus alerts us to opportunities that propel us forward. The clearer we are about our goals, the easier they will be to achieve. When we focus on the essence of what we want, we increase the range of possible ways for achieving our goals.

For example, if we want financial success, and we consider the essence of our goal, we may discover that what we are actually looking for is a creative challenge, or an opportunity to use our skills or knowledge, or respect from our family and friends. When we uncover and acknowledge what we want, we may find all sorts of ways in which our goals can be accomplished. When we are clear about our desire, it is easier to stay open to receive it, however it might come. We're less likely to limit ourselves to pursuing our dreams in a particular way. When we ask ourselves the question, "Can I have the essence of what I want right now?" we may discover that what we really wanted has already come to us and all we need to do is recognize it. The key is to focus on what you want—not on what you don't want. By picturing the essence of what you want, you direct your creative energies to create the desired reality.

Six years ago, I found that my hectic work and travel schedule often left me tired and drained. One day, I decided I was no longer willing to live my life that way. Instead, I wanted to feel refreshed both physically and mentally.

Over the next year, I lost thirty pounds by changing my eating habits and developing a daily exercise routine. Because I was focused on the essence of what I wanted—feeling refreshed—instead of on the mechanics of my goal, diet and exercise, it was much easier to stay committed to my purpose.

I started the day with an outdoor run in the fresh air, with the sun rising and the birds singing. I found both the activity and the environment invigorating and energizing. Most of the time I ran by myself. When others offered to join me, I usually declined because I saw my morning run as time for myself, without commitments, competition, or interaction.

After the run, I ate a breakfast of fresh fruit or fruit juices. I was absolutely amazed at how good freshly squeezed fruit juice tasted after a workout. Throughout the day, when I was tested by old eating patterns, I would consider the "refreshment value" of a piece of cake or a bag of French fries compared to my morning fruit juice. This perspective allowed me to decrease my desire for high-calorie foods and replace it with an appetite for more wholesome foods.

When I was strongly tempted, I would think about how refreshed and vibrant I would feel if I weighed the same as I had when I graduated from high school. Steadfastly holding onto the essence of my goal helped me stay focused on what I wanted and why.

Trust Yourself

Change is a process of developing a greater awareness, understanding, and knowledge of yourself. It can be a time of new experiences, learning, and growth, but it can also bring doubts to the surface as old beliefs and patterns block new understandings. When negative emotions occur, acknowledge them and pay attention to their occurrence. Ask yourself, "Why am I reacting this way? What can I learn from this? Where is the opportunity for growth in this situation?" Consciously work to replace negative emotional patterns with positive feelings that support your goal. Take action to solve small problems before they become big.

Remember, everything that happens can be used to advance your personal growth and achieve your goals. What you feel and how you respond are choices. As a result of prior conditioning or old habits, feelings may surface, but you can consciously shift your focus back to the essence of what you want and give yourself permission to feel differently. Decide to release your fears and let them go. Easier said than done, perhaps, but not impossible. All it takes is your willingness and your intention. You may not master this skill overnight, but each step you take is progress.

When I began to write this book, many doubts and fears surfaced. What am I going to say? What if the readers don't understand? What if they don't like it? Each question led me to think about myself—my beliefs, my ideas, my skills, and my experiences. When I acknowledged my fears and consciously chose to release my doubts, the pattern and structure of the book emerged.

Each question led me to a deeper understanding of the power within myself. I reminded myself to trust my inner voice and to recognize that each experience was saying something to me—each idea was a direction to explore and understand.

At first, looking inside myself for the answers was a journey into unfamiliar territory. I had no previous experience with this level of searching and questioning. I struggled to stay on track. At times, I wanted to give up and focus only on my consulting, but a voice inside kept urging me to stick with the writing project.

When colleagues, friends and family members asked questions that raised my doubts and fears, I had to remind myself that others could suggest thoughts, but I was the one who accepted or rejected them for myself. I was the one who decided what I believed. In order to cope, I focused on why the book was important to me—the essence of the goal—and reminded myself that this was a journey of learning and growing. I can remember saying during one particular conversation, "I don't know how this will turn out; I don't have a guarantee that it will be successful; all I know is that it is something I want to do right now."

Every moment is a new opportunity to make a fresh choice to move in a direction that is consistent with your goals, values and desires. Be true to yourself. Focus on the essence of what you want and believe in your own vision. When doubts and negative thoughts creep in, acknowledge what is happening and redirect your thoughts and energies to your higher purpose. Allow for mistakes and stay open to all possibilities. Every conscious choice is a step in the right direction.

What lies behind us and what lies before us
are tiny matters
compared to what lies within us.

—Ralph Waldo Emerson

We know the truth, not only by reason
but by the heart.

—Blaise Pascal

Some men see things as they are
and say "why?"
I dream of things that never were,
and say "why not?"

—George Bernard Shaw.

Chapter 3

Focus on What You Want

Imagination

There are no limits to what our minds can envision. Unfortunately, as adults, most of us have lost the innocence and spontaneity of childhood. As children, we thrived in the world of imagination—playing house or pretending we were a doctor, nurse, or astronaut. There were no limits to our world and we created hundreds of variations on the games and roles we played.

Granted, it's much simpler to play house than to be a real wife and mother or husband and father, and it's much easier to pretend we're a doctor or an astronaut than to gain admission to medical school or into the NASA program; but the same energy that makes dreams into realities for real-life doctors and astronauts, or mothers and fathers, is available to be utilized by all of us. If we tap into our childlike imagination, we will see beyond what is presently possible. Our imagination allows us to see a picture of something that does not yet exist. It also acts as a blueprint that directs our energies and opens us to new possibilities.

When a dream begins to take shape, it becomes a vision—a specific picture of something different, a new reality, that creates hope and gives us the courage to step into tomorrow. Without a vision, there is no basis for goals and, consequently no attainment.

The power of the dream drives visionaries to persist against obstacles and create their own opportunities to turn the vision into reality. When the existing system sought to stifle her vision of what education could be, Marva Collins, a second-grade teacher in Chicago, set out to create her own school—Westside Preparatory.

Collins believed her role as an educator was to help children develop character and to instill a positive self-image. She produced incredible results with students who were rejected by the public school as retarded or trouble-makers. She helped students who could not read simple sentences to read Shakespearean plays such as *Macbeth*. She instilled confidence and self-reliance by emphasizing excellence in each moment and each decision through constant practice. She devised her own methods and set a standard based on the philosophy that "all of us are looking for someone to insist that we be all that we can be."

Today her methods are known worldwide. A television movie was produced documenting her life; and through grants and sponsorship by people who believe in her dream, she has established a teacher-training institute which trains more than 1,800 teachers a year.

When we have vision, every experience becomes an opportunity to grow, learn, and move forward. When we keep our goals in mind, even failure or problems can be used to create success. Most people struggle to create the life they want because they haven't clearly defined where they want to go and they haven't visualized what it will be like when they get there.

Take a moment now and think honestly about your life. Are you excited? Is it working the way you want? Are you where you want to be? What makes you happy? How would you like your life to be different? Open your mind to new possibilities and give yourself permission to entertain unlimited thoughts and enjoy lofty expectations.

When I looked back over the years, I knew that even though I enjoyed my work and my career, there was something missing. On one level, I was successful and fulfilled, but I still wanted more. I wanted to have a greater impact somehow—to make a more profound difference in the world.

I began to ask myself questions like, "What is the purpose of my life? Why do I exist? Why am I here?" I knew intuitively that the answers to these questions would help me determine what was missing in my life. For a while, I struggled to find the answers and to identify what I wanted to accomplish with my life.

Along the way, I gained important insight into how our life's values determine our focus from Tony Robbins's book *Awaken the Giant Within*. Robbins explains how two people can have the same values but feel very differently about their lives because of the way they define their values.

To illustrate, he describes two men who both value success, but who have different definitions of how to succeed. The first man, a well-known Fortune

500 executive, didn't feel successful because he was not earning three million dollars a year, didn't have eight percent body fat, and was often frustrated with his children. When the other man was asked whether he was successful, he responded cheerfully, "Absolutely—every day above ground is a great day." The two men shared the same value, but the one who had limited his definition to externals was feeling frustrated and unfulfilled, while the man who was focused on the essence of what he wanted was feeling great.

This story led me to ask more questions about my life: What is important to me in life? My career? My job? My family? What would I like to do with my life? What excites me? What would I like to learn?

As I explored these questions, a pattern emerged. I recognized that the purpose of my life was to make a difference with people. But what did that really mean? And how did it apply to my work, career and life? I decided I could make a difference by being loving and supportive, by helping others learn and grow, and by helping organizations to be more supportive and caring.

As I looked at the above list, I realized that sometimes I would focus so hard on making a difference that I would forget to take care of myself—and the result was burnout. I knew I needed a set of values that empowered and supported myself as well as others. I developed the following list of hierarchical values:

- Love—to love myself and others.

- Health—to have the energy and strength to help others.

- Cheerfulness—to be grateful for my life and to see new possibilities.

- Growing and learning—to continue to stretch and try new experiences.

- Making a difference—to be loving and supportive, to help others learn and grow, and to help organizations become more supportive and caring.

Based on this list of values, I developed a life purpose statement, a daily code of conduct, and a code of truth (beliefs) as focal points to guide my decisions, attitudes and actions in ways consistent with my declared values.

Purpose

The purpose of my life is
to give and receive love
that empowers myself and others
to create a compelling future.

Code of Conduct

- *Friendly and outgoing*
- *Sensitive and supportive*
- *Playful and sharing*
- *Open and flexible*
- *Resourceful and congruent*
- *Risking and stretching*
- *Determined and focused*

Code of Truth

- *Everything happens for a reason and purpose*
- *There is always a way if I am committed*
- *I am master of my states*
- *I create my own reality and I am responsible for what I create*
- *Change happens in a moment*
- *Direction is more important than outcome*

Moving Toward Values

I am loving

> *Any time I*
> - am warm and supportive to others.
> - look for love in others.
> - remember the relationship is more important than the task.
> - remember the love I always have in my heart.
> - look for the playful child in myself and others.

I am healthy

> *Any time I*
> - treat my body with love and respect.
> - exercise.
> - acknowledge how great I feel.
> - am centered and balanced.
> - push my body to expand its present limits.

I am cheerful

> *Any time I*
> - focus on what I am grateful for in my life.
> - am open to new possibilities.
> - find pleasure and joy in the process.
> - clarify and take action on my goals.
> - let my child play.
> - focus on creating my life.

I am growing and learning

> *Any time I*
> - try something new.
> - learn from an experience.
> - stretch beyond my limits.
> - make new distinctions.
> - question the meaning of an experience.

I am making a difference

> *Any time I*
> - am loving and supportive.
> - help others learn and grow.
> - help organization systems change to be more supportive and caring.

To begin creating your own statements of purpose, values, and code of conduct and code of truth, think about your life and ask yourself the following questions:

- What is important to me in my life?

- What would I need to do to have what I want?

- What would I need to believe?

Maintain Your Focus

Your vision creates an internal standard that enables you to confront conflicting values and make continual adjustments. It acts as a symbolic reminder of what is important to you. As you compare your current reality to your vision, you create an impetus for action, which acts as a magnetic force to pull you forward. In a sense, your thoughts are like magnets that attract situations and opportunities to you.

Once your statements of purpose are in writing, begin to integrate your vision into your daily activities. Think about what you want and imagine (picture in your mind) achieving your goal. Think about why you want what you have identified and how good it will feel to accomplish your purpose.

At first, you might struggle to maintain your focus on your declared values. To help yourself, create simple reminders. Here are some things that I devised to help myself stay focused on my vision:

- Display your vision statement, values, and rules in your home and office. I hung a framed copy on my wall over my desk as a constant reminder of my purpose.

- Carry a copy with you. I made a laminated copy and carried it in my briefcase at all times. I used it to recenter myself when I was upset or frustrated.

- Use your statements as affirmations. I recited my purpose statement, code of conduct, and values to myself during my daily runs.

- Consciously live your values throughout the day. As the old saying goes, practice makes perfect. I decided that if I was truly committed to living my values, they needed to be visible. To create a climate of accountability, I displayed my purpose statement and my values in my office, where others could see them and hold me accountable when I wasn't living in accordance to my stated values.

At first my colleagues were uncertain how to respond to a statement like "My purpose is to give and receive love that empowers myself and others to create a compelling future." But over time, my actions demonstrated my commitment to my vision, which in turn led to many meaningful discussions.

- Review your vision daily. At the end of the day, I reflected on how I was living my values and progressing toward my goals. I identified areas to re-emphasize and created an intention of focus for the next day.

- Stay on track. Your vision directs your energies toward a goal, but your inner guidance is what enables you to determine whether you are still on the right path or whether the target needs adjustment. Intuition is your ability to know without words. It is a sense or feeling of rightness or understanding. Your intuition constantly sends you messages in the form of insights, new ideas or feelings. These bursts of intuition can occur at any time, while you're taking a walk, talking to someone, or engaged in an activity.

- Learn to trust your insights. Play with them. Be open to new possibilities or definitions, even if at that moment you see no way to carry them out. Allow the messages to flow freely to you without expectations of a specific answer. Identify possible interpretations or connotations; be curious and focus on expanding your horizons and learning. Notice which insights you take action on and which you do not. Record the results.

Make the Connection

All of us have an intuitive inner guidance system, but most of us have been taught to ignore or discount our feelings. We need to learn to reconnect with our internal self and retrain ourselves to listen to and pay attention to our feelings. Here are some simple steps to make the connection:

Relax. Take a few moments to quiet your mind. Take a deep breath and imagine yourself plugging into the outlet of your inner guidance system. Focus on feeling peaceful and relaxed. Become aware of your energy and thoughts. Allow your awareness to move into your body. Notice areas of tension or fatigue. Take a deep breath and visualize your breath flowing through and releasing the tension.

Ask a question and expect an answer. Ask a question such as "What do I need to know right now?" or "Is this part of my path right now?" or "What direction do I need to take right now?" Once you have asked the question, let go of your reactive self and be open to receive answers from your intuition. Notice what thoughts, feelings or images come to you.

Trust your impressions. A message may occur immediately, or it may come later in an unexpected way—in a comment from a friend or a newspaper article. Remember, all things happen for a reason, and each message has significance. Learn to trust and act on your insights. When you have the urge to do something, do it! If you do not receive a clear message, continue throughout the day to be aware of your thoughts or feelings and be open to receive new inputs. Suspend disbelief and adopt a mind-set for receiving help. Trust that your inner messages are leading you toward your goals.

Practice using your intuition. Increase your trust in the messages by practicing daily in simple, routine situations. For example, before making a phone call, take a moment to go within and ask if this is a good time to call; or before accepting a dinner invitation, use your intuition to check out your response. Play with it, have fun and notice how much easier it becomes to tap into your inner guidance system.

Nothing happens unless first a dream.

—Carl Sandburg

*There are no limitations to the mind,
except those we acknowledge.*

—Napoleon Hill

*Men do not attract that which they want,
but that which they are.*

—James Allen

Chapter 4

Magnetize Your Dreams

Step into the Future

Our thoughts have the power to transform our experience of reality. By directing our thoughts through the process of visualization, we can create an inner reality so powerful that it can change our external conditions. We can create our own virtual reality by imaging the desired state and experiencing the situation through our five senses.

Our imagination is not limited by time or space. It can be used to create fear, as when worrying about saying the wrong thing or losing our jobs, or it can be used to create what we want—success and happiness. Why not use the power of your imagination to condition yourself to achieve your goals?

Visualization is the process of creating an image in our minds. It is the process of directing and controlling our energies. As we mentally picture what we want to create, we are working with the energy of visualization. As we focus on the parts of life that we want to experience, we start living it. In a sense, our future creates our present. For example, you may want to experience more harmony and peace. By picturing yourself in harmony and peace, you become more centered and peaceful.

The more you work with your visualizations, the easier it will be to magnetize what you want. The more details you can identify and the more you associate with the image, the greater your possibility of success.

Everyone possesses the power of imagination. Every sensation we have ever experienced is recorded in our brains. We have the ability to recall past experiences as vividly as the first time we saw them. This image is a mental representation of our five-sense reality.

Whenever we recall an image, we can reproduce the same feelings we experienced during the initial interaction. We can produce emotional states and physiological responses. For example, imagine eating a lemon. Do you instantly have a reaction? Can you feel your mouth tighten and produce saliva? Many of my clients complain that they can't visualize or that they have poor imaginations. The real problem is that they have not learned to effectively direct their imaginations.

Visualization is not some esoteric mind game. It is actually the natural process of memory. It is how we remember sensations and use them to recreate an image of what was experienced. Take a moment now and look around your environment. Focus your eyes on one particular object, such as a chair or table, and notice all of its details—its shape, size, color, texture. Close your eyes and picture the object in your mind, Re-create all the details you can remember. Now, open your eyes and check the details. Close your eyes again and create the image once more. Do this a few times and notice how it becomes easier to picture the object in your mind. In the same way that exercising a muscle increases its strength, if we exercise our imaginations we will build our mental strength and agility.

Images become more vivid with practice. Practice daily to increase your awareness and sensitivity by noticing the sights and sounds around you. Become aware of the changes in your environment and notice the effects of those changes. Increase your skills daily and have fun!

Here are some suggestions for creating powerful images:

- Develop your skills of observation by playing an awareness game where your goal is to notice and remember one item each time you walk into a room.

- Increase your sensory skills by going for a walk and noticing the sights and sounds. Look at the size and shapes of trees, and the texture and design of the buildings. Observe the light patterns in the sky and listen to the sounds of birds singing, children playing, or people talking. Or go to a shopping mall and observe the design and color of the window displays and advertisements, or sit and watch the people go by.

- Practice simple visualizations by taking a few moments each day to draw a mental picture of an object. Carefully observe the object, then close your eyes and picture it in your mind.

- Practice detailed visualizations by recalling images like the warmth of the sun on your back as you walk along a beach with the waves rolling and crashing. Try to visualize as many details as possible to create the feeling of being in the experience.

- Anchor your images by linking them to real life objects that you encounter daily. For example, I visualize the lights going on all over the city as the sun sets. Each light represents a person affected by my work. Whenever I travel and see the lights of a city, I remind myself that each light represents my work.

- Experiment and change your visualizations by experimenting with your internal representations. To make my images as real as possible, I imagine an instrument panel or keyboard that controls the sights, sounds and feelings of my visualization.

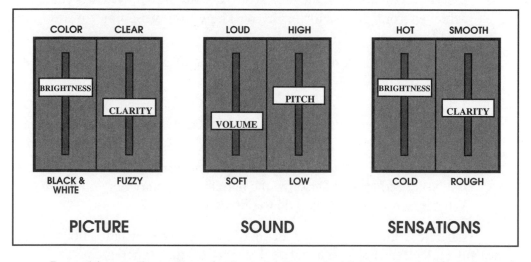

I use this panel to adjust the images. Does the picture need to be brighter? Do the sounds need to be louder or softer? Do the sensations need to change? I adjust the dials until I create the exact picture I want.

Build Your Own Virtual Reality

Visualizations are mental rehearsals that can be used to prepare for upcoming events. Imaging provides a way to step into the future and experience it now. The more real and vivid the imaginary experience, the easier it is to re-create it in your daily life. The most important aspect of your visualization is to see yourself in the present accomplishing your goals. Make sure that you see the image through your own eyes, not through the eyes of a spectator.

To produce the desired results, precisely map out the situation you want to create. As your images become more vivid, their power to create positive change will be enhanced. Describe as clearly and specifically as possible your present situation and what you would like to change.

To produce the desired results, practice the following steps:

1. State the desired outcome in positive terms. Specifically what do you want? What does this mean? Why is it important?

2. Specify the present situation. Where are you now?

3. Specify the outcome. What will you see, hear, and feel when you have it?

4. Identify evidence of achievement. How will you know when you have achieved your goal? How will you know you are going toward your goal?

5. What will be the result of your achievement? What will this outcome get for you or allow you to do?

6. What prevents you from experiencing your desired outcome now? Write down anything that you think might prevent you from achieving your goals.

7. What will you need to believe in order to accomplish your goals? How will you need to act? Describe the beliefs and behaviors you will need. What specifically will you do to pursue your goal?

Associate with the experience. In order for your visualizations to be powerful and effective, you must feel a part of the experience—as if the situation were happening right now. One of the best ways to enhance your images and amplify your experience is to link the visualization to physical movement. Imagine the situation and physically step into it by practicing the following steps:

1. Select a particular situation—for example, being confident and effective in a job interview.

2. Create a resourceful space by locating an area in front of you and visualizing an imaginary border around it, such as a circle.

3. Think about the situation or experience. Visualize the situation and associate with it as if you were right there engaging in the experience. See exactly what you would see if you were really there. Notice the

sights, sounds, colors, and textures. For example, picture yourself getting ready for the interview, looking great in a new outfit, feeling relaxed and confident, and moving steadily to get ready. Then see yourself arriving a few minutes early to park the car and go into the office.

4. Step forward into the resourceful space and maintain your visualization. Notice your surroundings—the plants, pictures, and other people in the room. See yourself walking confidently and smiling at the receptionist as you announce your arrival for your appointment. See yourself smiling and walking into the interview room to shake hands with the interviewer. Confidently sit down and answer the first few questions. Notice yourself relaxing and enjoying the discussion as it continues. Become aware of how easy it is to answer the questions. See yourself shaking hands to leave. As you walk out, picture yourself feeling relaxed and confident.

5. Step out of your resourceful place. Observe the interaction as if you were seeing it from the point of view of someone outside of the situation. Observe your own behavior. If you could do it again what would you do differently? Which questions would you answer differently? Would any of your gestures change? Now put yourself inside the other person's role—imagine you were in the interviewer's shoes. How would you experience your behavior from that perspective?

6. Repeat the process by once again stepping into the resourceful space, and visualize the situation again; but this time use the knowledge of what to do differently. Replay the entire situation and then step out of the space.

Repeat this visualization twice daily until you have conditioned yourself to respond automatically and have positively programmed yourself to achieve your goal. The more clear and distinct the image, the easier it will be to create what you want. You can increase the power of your images by becoming more aware of your surroundings and sensations as well as practicing your visualization skills.

Attract What You Want

Suspend disbelief. What you believe or don't believe creates your reality. The only limits on what you can have are the limits you create. In order to attract what you want, you must open your mind to the possibility of your dreams becoming reality. Once you have made this decision, what you want begins to unfold to the degree you are open to receive.

Understand the power of words. What you talk about reveals your inner perspective. What you say creates your reality. Everything you say impacts your experience. Your subconscious mind hears your words and goes to work to make what you say come true.

A few years ago, I worked in a company that was downsizing. I decided to become more aware of the words that impacted my daily experience. I began to play with my vocabulary to accentuate the positive and de-emphasize the negative.

I was amazed when I observed my own responses and the reactions of others. I started out by changing my reply to a morning greeting. Whenever someone said, "Good morning. How are you?" instead of saying "Fine," I decided to respond by saying "Great."

If I was feeling tired or upset, saying the word "great" gave me a lift. Soon I *was* feeling great! Later I changed my response to "Super," and I immediately noticed an interesting effect on others.

I could see the wheels turning as my coworkers tried to make sense of this non-normal response. Often individuals would stop for a brief moment, pull back and analyze the response. Hearing "super" interrupted their automatic pilot pattern and started them thinking.

I continued to play with the words I used and found that when I talked about a problem as a "challenge," the energy of the situation changed. Challenges were lighter and easier to handle than problems, and my focus shifted to the possibility of a solution.

Once I understood the power of words, I became more sensitive not only to the words I used but also to the words used by people around me. I noticed how my experience was framed by what was said. I noticed how some words energized people while other words sapped their energy. I noticed that when I described myself as "a bit concerned" instead of "anxious," I was calmer and more open to the moment. When I reframed my emotions, by changing "overwhelmed" to simply "puzzled," I became more resourceful. Puzzles are made for solving, whereas overwhelming circumstances are debilitating.

Before you dismiss what I'm saying as "mere semantics," consider this: My words ultimately defined my experience of reality, not the other way around. When I characterized a "challenge" as "puzzling," rather than succumbing to an "overwhelming problem, I found that I truly was not overwhelmed and I had fewer problems. Instead, my mind was genuinely challenged to solve an interesting puzzle.

Begin today, to notice the words you use and the feelings that develop. Become aware of disempowering words like "can't," "try," "must," "have to," or "should" which emphasize that the situation is out of your control. By exchanging these words for more empowering options—such as "will," "want to," "choose to," or "desire," or by eliminating them from your vocabulary, you create a shift from external power to the power of choice.

Similar energy attracts. Our thoughts are like magnets, drawing situations and opportunities toward us. Our thoughts create an energy field in all directions that precedes us wherever we go. They magnetize similar emotions from the people around us. If our thoughts are negative, we will attract everyone in the room who is feeling the same emotional energy. Conversely, if we have a positive picture of something and are certain it will happen, we will attract that situation to ourselves.

Often our external experiences are a mirror of our inner selves. We experience whatever our inner selves project. We can learn to be aware of our own energy by becoming aware of the energy of those around us. If we find ourselves surrounded by negative people, it gives us a clue to our own inner negativity. When we consciously choose a more positive expression of ourselves, we will attract others who share our positive outlook.

Notice the words that other people use, how they hold their bodies and the sound of their voices. By focusing on what we see and hear, we can become aware of our own actions. Have you ever noticed your voice getting louder when the other person raises hers?

When we recognize our energy and the energy around us, we can make a conscious choice to change the direction of that energy. We can choose which thoughts and feelings we are willing to tune into. Whenever you go into a place and notice that you are feeling uncomfortable or negative—stop—take a deep breath and think about how you want to feel. Make a conscious choice to feel different and visualize yourself feeling that way.

Experiment with your magnetic energy. You can consciously work with your energy and thoughts to create the experience of reality that you want. By focusing on and imagining the life that you want to create, you can produce a magnetic force that draws it to you. You can work with the energies to open up the space and increase your readiness to receive.

Learn to play and experiment with your internal energy by visualizing an energy keyboard similar to the one you used to create powerful images. Adjust the dials to create the exact picture and levels of energy required to magnetize the world around you and attract the experiences you desire.

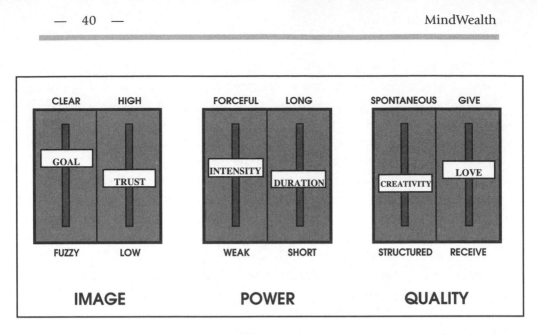

CLEAR	HIGH	FORCEFUL	LONG	SPONTANEOUS	GIVE
GOAL	TRUST	INTENSITY	DURATION	CREATIVITY	LOVE
FUZZY	LOW	WEAK	SHORT	STRUCTURED	RECEIVE
IMAGE		**POWER**		**QUALITY**	

Use the following procedure to experiment with your magnetic energy:

1. Sit quietly, relax, and think about what you want to magnetize. Be as specific as possible about the functions, features or feelings that you would like to attract.

2. Visualize a picture of yourself receiving what you want. Imagine that you have a power source within you—an energy ball—that generates and radiates energy. See the energy radiating out through your body and into the scene.

3. Focus your thoughts on what you want to magnetize and adjust the energy ball to whatever size you think it needs to be to attract what you want. Play with the size, shape and intensity of the ball by adjusting the dials of the keyboard.

4. Clarify your goals and refine the details of your vision. Adjust the level of your beliefs, openness and willingness to trust your intuition. Fine-tune your internal energy—flow, vibration, duration and intensity. Focus on the specific qualities you want to create—harmony, peace, love, prosperity. Continue to modify the energy until it feels right. As you adjust the levels, you are creating a magnetic force field.

5. Continue to generate energy as long as it feels easy and right. Stop magnetizing when you notice the energy beginning to fall.

The more you play with your visualizations, the more immediately conscious and deliberate they will become and the easier it will be to create the desired outcomes. As you clarify specific details of your vision, you create an awareness and focus that enables you to take advantage of opportunities as they appear.

Go with the Flow

Don't force your visualizations. Instead, *allow* them to take shape. Remain open to new possibilities for *how* your dreams will be accomplished. If you push too hard, you will repel the very things you seek, because the energy you use will be based on fear and anxiety. Open yourself to the flow of possibilities by acknowledging your fears and letting go of preconceived ideas. Be open to creative new ways to get what you want by living in the present and being yourself. Believe you deserve to have the best and trust your ideas. Persist in implementing them. Do whatever your intuition indicates, then surrender and trust that whatever happens is for your greatest good.

Today's actions create tomorrow's future. Ask yourself, "What is the most important action I can take today? What steps can I implement now?" If you do not know how to do something, act as if you did. Pretend to accomplish the things you desire. Your subconscious mind does not know the difference between what is imagined and what is actually happening. By simply focusing on what you want, intending to have it, and acting as if it were already here, your inner guidance system will direct and lead you each step of the way.

The future belongs to those who believe in the beauty of their dreams.

—Eleanor Roosevelt

In the middle of difficulty lies opportunity.

—Albert Einstein

Nothing can bring peace but yourself.

—Ralph Waldo Emerson

Chapter 5

Create Consistent Thoughts and Actions

Establish Balance

Achieving the life you want requires an integration of thoughts and actions. Integration is a process of creating an internal stability or balance that enables you to trust your ability to handle each situation. Balance enables you to

- go with the flow, yet retain control of direction.
- be flexible and yet take advantage of your emotional energy.
- maintain emotional equilibrium while expressing deep feelings.

Can you imagine what your life would be like if you always felt calm, centered and balanced? Balance is a blending of mental and physical energy to create an inner harmony and stability that supports and nurtures your growth. You can create balance by implementing the following seven steps:

B	Between opposites, find equilibrium
A	Align your energy
L	Lighten the load
A	Access answers from within
N	Nurture yourself
C	Create opportunities
E	Elicit effortless energy

Between Opposites, Find Equilibrium

Every situation is made up of qualities that are equal and opposite but cannot exist independently of each other. Each quality complements the other and strengthens it by contrast. For example, the qualities of light and darkness are equal opposites. Light is experienced in its contrast to darkness. Likewise, confidence exists in contrast to fear, and stillness is the absence of movement. Each moment is created by the flow between opposites. When light increases, darkness decreases; when confidence increases, fear decreases. Internal balance is created by adjusting the flow. We achieve balance in our lives when we discover the point of equilibrium in a situation that fits into our vision for how the moment will unfold.

Align Your Energy

Aligning our energy is a process of creating harmony within ourselves and then acting in accordance with our inner peace. Alignment occurs when we fully experience the moment, acknowledge what is happening around us and within us, and then adjust our inner qualities to support our visions. For example, we can make a conscious choice to flow from uncertainty to certainty, fear to confidence, reaction to response, control to openness, continuity to change, or stillness to action.

Lighten the Load

Don't feed your fears. Don't waste energy denying your feelings. Let go of irrelevant thoughts and worries. Listen to your intuition, and once you've decided on an action, don't waste energy worrying about the result. Close the door on the past and maintain your agility in the present moment.

Access Answers from Within

Emotions of serenity and peace come from knowing that what you feel is a choice. You have the ability to feel the way you want at all times. When a negative emotion occurs, redirect and harness your energy by focusing on what you want to feel. Notice your feelings moment by moment and ask yourself questions like, "What would I like to feel right now? How can I feel differently? What is important for me to do?"

Nurture Yourself

Set aside time for just "being." Have no agenda other than to be fully present and experience the moment totally. Develop a daily habit of taking time for yourself. You may want to sit and reflect, walk in nature, listen to music, or meditate. Do whatever feels right for you. This is your time!

Create Opportunities

Look at your life from a higher viewpoint and see how the events of your life fit together. The cycle of change is never-ending, but there is a season for everything. There is a time for preparing the land, a time for planting the seed, a time for fertilizing and nurturing the plants, and a time for harvesting the crop. Recognizing the cyclical nature of change helps us avoid accepting negative conditions as permanent. We can view uncertainty as a challenge and opportunity—a time of new possibilities.

Elicit Effortless Energy

Maintaining balance allows us to tap into the natural energy within ourselves. Balance, or equilibrium, is the power point where we can be totally immersed in an activity without thoughts of the past or future. We live in a society that equates effort with striving—using power and strength to make something happen. You've heard the saying, "No pain, no gain." But what if it were possible to direct our energies with ease instead of effort?

The first step is to focus our attention on what we want and to be totally absorbed in concentration. Focus creates a heightened state of awareness where we can notice what is happening without reacting to it.

We have a natural ability to focus effectively on anything that is of interest to us. When we are interested or engaged, our attention is effortless. An attitude of curiosity creates the desire to know more. As soon as we admit the possibility of a new perspective, we open our attention effortlessly in another direction. Our effort becomes ease. Our ability to reflect about what is happening rather than reacting is an important skill that helps us create balance in the moment.

Energy Skills

Reflection is a process of seeing what "is," without distortion from our own thoughts. Reflection gives us insight into how our feelings are created by our mind-set—how we are framing the situation. This is a process of becoming aware of our predominant physical and mental states by observing habitual thought patterns and emotional triggers.

How can we gain this level of awareness? By giving ourselves permission to be still and observe. Take a moment to check in with you inner self and ask, "What am I thinking now?" Tune into your body by feeling your breath. Let your breath bring you back to the present moment. Keep your mind open and observe the moment without trying to change it. Become aware of any images, sensations or insights that surface. Use these emerging ideas to guide and direct your actions.

Stillness provides the opportunity for us to become aware of our thoughts in the present moment. When we sit still and observe our thoughts, we quickly realize how much our minds chatter in an internal monologue of desires, judgments, doubts, fears, and criticisms.

We believe we are in control of our minds, yet in moments of silence we discover that our minds are often running on their own. This river of consciousness affects every aspect of our lives: our relationships, our health, and our sense of purpose. These free-flowing thoughts and associations are useful when we are being creative, but uncontrolled thoughts that focus on fear and create doubts limit our capability to create the lives we want.

I've noticed that when I become fearful, my thoughts can quickly gain momentum to find more reasons to support my fears. Soon unrelated fears surface, and before long my fears have snowballed into an avalanche. At times like these, I make a conscious decision to stop and focus on what is good about the situation and what I can learn from it. This deliberate step enables me to shift my thoughts and refocus my energy.

We have conditioned ourselves to engage in thought. When we worry about something or wish for something else to happen, we believe we need to think about these issues. Often these thoughts confuse our awareness of what is happening at the present moment. When we find ways to quiet our minds, a new level of awareness can occur.

Confidence is an attitude that demonstrates that true power comes from within. It is the power of self-control—either you control yourself (your focus, emotions, state of consciousness), or you abdicate control to others.

Fear is part of our survival instinct. When something threatens our well-being, the fight-or-flight response is initiated to respond to the immediate danger. However, there are times when anxiety is generated by our imagination and fed by our interpretations of our experiences. These fears come from anticipating the unknown, creating doubt, uncertainty and frantic action. Our impulse toward action wastes energy and depletes resources. Moving beyond fear requires a redirection of our personal energy.

Often fear is acted out in subtle ways. A supervisor overmanages by controlling and focusing on minute details of a task; a manager constantly changes directions, with projects started, stopped, and restarted without a cohesive sense of vision; or an individual avoids facing his fear by staying constantly busy.

If you are working outside your sphere of influence, or feel overextended, retreat into the power within yourself. Take a moment to focus on your central purpose or vision—the essence of what you want. Then practice single-mindedness of purpose by focusing totally on the task at hand. Acknowledge your fears and then let them go—at least for the moment. You can always go back to your fears; don't waste energy denying or blocking them.

Above all, don't feed your fears. Remember, every situation is temporary. Decide on a course of action and listen to your inner wisdom. Once you decide to take the first step, the next step will become clear.

Thought and Action Integration

Clear your emotions by identifying and letting go of emotional blocks. Acknowledge what you are feeling by listing all your thoughts, feelings, assumptions, and beliefs about the situation. Ask yourself, "What emotions or feelings are blocking me from having what I want? What am I willing to give up?"

Quiet your mind by taking a step back and detaching yourself from the situation. Reframe your perspective by asking, "What is good about this situation? What can I learn from this? What emotions or feelings do I choose to release?"

Ground your energy by making a conscious connection between yourself and the physical space around you. Grounding can allow you to focus more on the present moment and help you to stabilize and balance your energy. It enhances your ability to feel whole or connected, confident, and focused. Ground your energy using the following process:

- Visualize a grounding cord—a hollow, flowing cord attached from the base of your spine to the center of the Earth.

- Release negative emotions down the cord. Visualize them flushing out of your system.

- Choose the feelings you want to have and visualize the situation the way you want it.

Center your energy and change your pattern of focus. Ask empowering questions such as "What can I learn from this?" "Can I remember a time I was anxious and it worked out?" "What is good about this situation?" Change by moving physically—walk, stand up, or change your actions.

Consciously choose a new direction and decide on the next step. Take a deep breath, look inside yourself, and ask "Where do I focus?" or "What do I do next?" Note any image words that come to mind. Trust your intuition and continue to reflect until you have a sense of a next step.

Establish your intention. State specifically what you intend to achieve or accomplish, and decide to have it. Consciously choose to change. Take appropriate action. Observe what happens and adjust accordingly.

Hold fast to the great image,
and all the world will come.

—Tao Te Ching

The privilege of a lifetime is being who you are.

—Joseph Campbell

Experience is not what happens to a man,
it is what a man does with
what happens to him.

—Aldous Huxley

Chapter 6

Celebrate Success

Honor Your Achievements

We've all heard that life is a journey, not a destination, yet we often tend to focus on the end result—winning the prize. Through TV shows, adulation of sports heroes, and our reward systems in schools and other organizations, our society constantly reinforces an emphasis on winning.

The drive to win affects the way we live our lives, the dreams to which we aspire, and the level of happiness we achieve. It sets up a paradigm that creates an either/or situation. If we don't win, we lose. Consequently, when our expectations are not fulfilled, we quickly focus on the negative—on what went wrong rather than on what we have learned or how far we have progressed.

The win/lose paradigm produces a constant dissatisfaction and a sense of not measuring up. I often notice this attitude in my work with individuals and teams. When I ask people to describe their strengths and weaknesses, they describe two or three times as many weaknesses as strengths. They often struggle even to identify their strengths.

When we define success as "progress" or "lessons learned," and consciously choose to celebrate our successes, we create moments that give deeper meaning to our lives. Honoring our achievements is a process of acknowledging who we are and what we have done. Each celebration helps to build self-esteem, create energy, and inspire us to a new level of success. Celebration opens the heart and frees the spirit.

Celebration is a recognition of who we are and an acknowledgment that we deserve the life we have chosen to live. It is a time to treat ourselves to joy and to give ourselves a special gift: time to relax and revitalize.

One of the things I do to celebrate success is give myself little gifts each day. Whenever possible, I watch a river or a waterfall, listen to the sounds, and observe the motion. I defocus my eyes and see the patterns of the water swirl, turn and travel their paths of least resistance. Within moments, I am in a relaxed, meditative state that revitalizes my energy.

Other times, I walk through nature and look at the shapes of the plants and observe the power of creation. As I walk along, I focus on the meaning each of these designs depicts. Taking time apart from the rigors of my work allows me to develop clarity regarding issues of the day.

Even if I have no opportunity to take a walk or watch a waterfall, I take time throughout the day to center myself and restore balance. It may be only a brief moment where I look at a picture of a mountain scene or visualize a waterfall and take a few deep breaths, but these moments add up to a pattern of balance and harmony.

Reward yourself with something special. If I'm heavily involved in a project or traveling on business, I reward myself with something special and out of the ordinary. I may go to the theater or experience a new sight in the city I'm visiting.

As a consultant, I travel to a lot of different places, yet I often only see airports, hotels, and conference centers. A few years ago I decided to give myself a gift by adopting the rule that whenever possible I would see something unique in each city I visited. Even if I have only an hour, I will arrange to see something that is uniquely part of that city's culture—a museum, an art gallery, or a historic site. Sometimes it takes seven or eight visits before I become familiar with a city, but each visit promises a special moment.

To commemorate special occasions like Christmas, I give myself a special gift—something I have always wanted but have not yet received. Sometimes I buy something big and expensive, and other times I choose something inexpensive but nonetheless satisfying. Sometimes it's functional and practical, and other times it is just something I know I will enjoy. Each gift, big or small, is a celebration of who I am and has significant meaning for me.

Take a moment now and think about the gift you would like to receive. Remember, this is a special gift for you, so have fun thinking about it, planning to have it, and getting it.

The second part of honoring achievements is accepting and recognizing the progress as it occurs. Acknowledge your growth, the lessons you've learned and the forward movement you have made. It can be as easy as asking yourself each day, "What did I learn today?" or in the moment asking, "What have I done well?" or "How is my life different than a year ago?"

Each question allows us a brief time to pause and reflect on what has occurred. It helps us to realign and refocus on what is important to us. It allows us to open ourselves to feelings of gratitude and to a new perspective.

Recommit to the Next Level

Embrace the changes in your life by taking the time to reflect on each question and writing your answers in a journal. Over time, your progress journal will become a record of your thoughts, dreams, desires and actions. It will help you to clarify what you want in life and to work out a blueprint for where you are going.

A progress journal opens a direct path for self-exploration and discovery. Writing down your discoveries and insights anchors your commitment to taking conscious control of your life. Your progress journal will help you to step back and clarify confusing feelings and beliefs. It will become a record of successes that you can use as a reference in new situations. Recording your progress will inspire you to achieve the life you want.

Reclaim Your Personal Power

The following diagram summarizes the six steps to reclaiming your personal power. Each step supports the others, and together they create a foundation for team and organizational power. Make a copy of this diagram and put it over your desk at work or on your refrigerator door—someplace where it can be a reminder and an inspiration to you. This visual cue card can help you to focus on the decisions and choices you are making from moment to moment and prompt you to ask questions about what you want to create in your life.

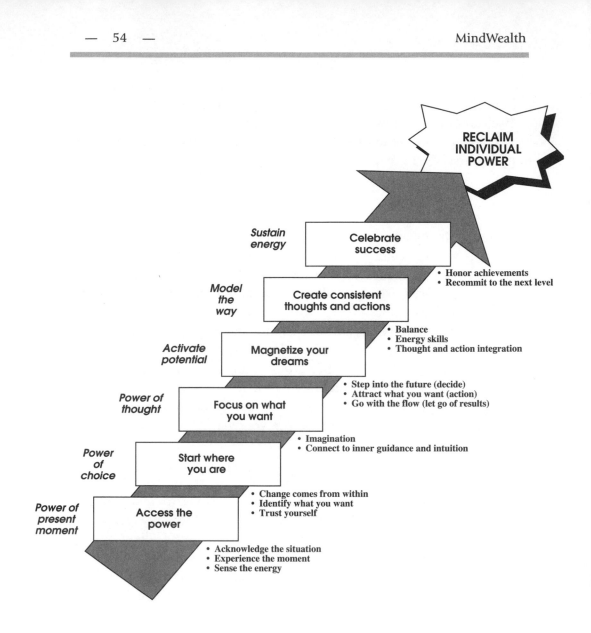

Real happiness comes from the things that cannot be taken away from you.

—John Wooden

Part II

Unleash Team Knowledge

We cannot become what we need to be
by remaining what we are.

—Max DePree

Purpose is the engine that powers our lives.

—Dennis Waitley

Chapter 7

A New Way of Being

Corporate Energy

As we gain deliberate control of our consciousness, we can begin to influence those around us in ways consistent with our values and vision. As more individuals become aware of their personal energy, they can significantly impact the collective consciousness or energy of a group, team, or organization.

Corporate energy is the combined equation of all the individual energy within an organization. In the same way that individual consciousness is the combination of a person's thoughts, beliefs, attitudes, and responses, corporate consciousness describes the thoughts, beliefs, attitudes and actions that characterize an organization. Corporate consciousness or energy denotes the system of shared values and beliefs that defines the company's management style and shapes the day-to-day behaviors of its employees. It is the informal rules that spell out how people are expected to act ("the way we do things here"). It depicts what the company stands for, and what management pays attention to, and it acts as a standard for decision making. In a way, corporate consciousness could be defined as an organization's sense of identity.

Because corporate energy derives from a blending of individual energies, we must understand that this energy occurs in patterns; these patterns reflect the whole system; this energy is constantly changing and transforming; and change in one part influences other parts.

Energy occurs in patterns. Corporate energy is a pattern of connectedness. We cannot consider one element without understanding how it relates to every other element. Everything that happens is as a result of other things that have already occurred, and every occurrence lays the foundation for the next step. When we seek to change or influence corporate energy, we must take into consideration all the interrelated ramifications. As we start to make changes, we must recognize that a particular incident may be a symptom of a larger issue. For example, conflict within a work team may be a reflection of conflict in top management.

Patterns reflect the whole system. Each pattern is a reflection of the whole system. Every circumstance or situation is like a drop of water that has its own separate identity, but when it joins thousands of other drops it creates the ocean.

Energy is constantly changing and transforming. Corporate consciousness is dynamic and flowing. Like ocean waves, it constantly recedes and starts over. By recognizing and focusing on the energy patterns in a given situation, we can influence what is happening by harmonizing our personal energy with the corporate energy or changing its direction.

For example, we might walk into a meeting and notice that the conversation is focused on worries, concerns, and what is not working well. We could transform the energy from a negative focus to a more empowering positive focus by joining the conversation and asking, "What is the opportunity in this situation? What can we learn from this? What can we do better?"

Change in one part influences other parts. Changing the energy in one area affects the energy in other areas. For example, our personal goals affect where we focus our attention. By changing our goals, we change our focus. Thus, each component affects the other. For an organizational change effort to succeed, it must account for the impact it has on subsystems. If a company moves into a new type of product, it may require not only a new marketing strategy but also change in the company reward system to support the strategy.

High Voltage Power Pack

Unleashing the power within the organization requires tapping into the hidden potential of the organization and redirecting employees' values from old commitments to new. The stronger and more distinctive the culture, the more important it is to match changes to the organization's climate. For integration to occur, a supportive internal culture must be developed by understanding individual energy patterns and creating an awareness of the necessity to change.

Start where the system is. Before we can decide to harmonize ourselves with the corporate energy or seek to redirect it, we must gain a clear understanding of the present situation. Take time to observe your own energy and the energy around you. Ask yourself, "What do I notice right now? What could be done differently, or what could *I* do differently?"

Everything is data. When we set aside our preconceived notions of what should or should not happen in a situation, we open ourselves to awareness of the present moment. In the present moment, we can observe or sense the energy within and around us, and all of this input is data that can be used to evaluate our options and choose the appropriate response for the moment. For example, we might walk into a room and notice that no one is talking. This silence might indicate that people are tired or disinterested, or we may have walked in at an inopportune moment in a meeting. The key to applying the data is to be aware of each moment by encountering each moment as a new beginning—letting go of our previous thoughts or beliefs about the situation and simply observing what is occurring in the moment. We can deliberately awaken ourselves to the moment by asking ourselves questions, like "What is happening right now?" or "What can I learn from this?"

As you learn how to reclaim your personal power and begin to focus on what you want—and as you magnetize your dreams—you will begin to discover opportunities to influence others—family, friends and coworkers. When individuals unleash their personal power within a group, a new synergy—with unlimited potential—is created. Tapping into the four voltages of team energy unlocks the power of the team. Together these four energy sources create a high voltage power pack.

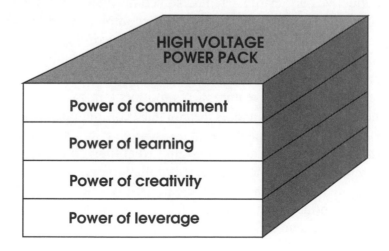

HIGH VOLTAGE
POWER PACK

Power of commitment

Power of learning

Power of creativity

Power of leverage

Power of commitment. This is the process of aligning individual energies by connecting all team activities to a common purpose. Commitment draws together the assets of ownership, interdependence and integration within the team.

Power of learning. This is the power to transfer skills and knowledge to new situations. Learning allows the team to let go of "the way it has always been done," and brings a fresh approach to thoughts, beliefs, and procedures. It is the ability to acknowledge what you know and don't know and to refocus the individual energies within the group.

Power of creativity. This is the power of transformation. It is the process of exploring options and allowing ideas to come that produce new and different experiences.

Power of leverage. This is the process of creating a competitive advantage by translating a group's unique skills and abilities into a distinctive basis of differentiation.

Turning on this high-voltage power pack requires a new way of being—a team based on partnership instead of hierarchy—with trust, openness, sharing and a common purpose.

Partnership

A true partnership occurs when every individual is respected for his or her presence and contribution. Relationships are based on similar values and beliefs, as well as a commitment to support and enhance each other—to contribute, grow, and learn.

In an effective partnership, each person contributes to a common purpose to create something more than they could accomplish working as individuals—the value of the whole is greater than the sum of the parts. In order for a partnership to work, the common purpose must be mutually identified and agreed upon—never imposed.

Powerful partnerships require a commitment from each individual to stick together through rough times. Partners must communicate their needs and actively evaluate the part each plays in co-creating every situation—standing up for what they believe, yet acknowledging what they don't know.

The strength of a partnership lies in collaboration, a rhythmic river of flowing energy that changes and evolves. In the give and take of group inter-actions, the truly collaborative team member will strive for what she wants, yet at the same time evaluate the ideas of others and be prepared to do something different. Partnerships move forward on the delicate balance between the enlightened self-interest of individuals and their willingness to let go and create space for another person to develop.

Trust

Trust is the cornerstone of every partnership. Without trust, the walls of cooperative activity collapse, causing chaos and confusion. Mutual support and trust is created by actions, not by words. Trust is based on our perception of ourselves and others. It's a feeling or sense that we can count on another person to support us under adverse conditions without taking advantage of us.

Trust is not automatic—it takes time to build. And the construction process can be very delicate. Trust can never be coerced, only earned. Trust springs from a willingness to be vulnerable with another person, by openly sharing feelings and communicating authentically in the moment. This requires honest feedback that honors the individual.

When group members know where they stand with each other and individual ideas are accepted and feelings acknowledged, trust is strengthened. When a high level of trust has been achieved, the following team assets are made available:

- appropriate risk-taking
- spontaneity
- creativity
- collaboration
- self-trust

Openness

Partnership doesn't mean that everyone necessarily shares the same viewpoint. On the contrary, diversity of perspective is one of the strong points of team dynamics. Partnerships are weakened when group members "go along" to avoid "making waves." True partnership requires working through differences by letting go of fear and judgment and disclosing our feelings in the moment.

Sharing feelings and intentions allows for interaction at a different level. People get to know each other—their dreams, aspirations, and concerns. Feedback is shared for awareness and for ongoing course correction.

As sharing continues to grow and develop, people are able to see beyond their own self-interest to a higher vision or common purpose. For this synergy to occur, we need both a safe environment, where one may speak openly, and the skills to effectively evaluate our perceptions and thinking.

Establish Ground Rules

It is often hard to admit difficulties to others unless you trust them and believe that they will not take advantage of what you have told them. Admitting our weaknesses may be easy with a friend, but it is harder with our bosses, subordinates, or colleagues.

To create a safe environment, group guidelines must be developed to govern the use of information. Team members need to feel comfortable and confident that information disclosed within the group will not be criticized or put down, but rather accepted and acknowledged on its own merits.

Ground rules set the boundaries for creating a positive, healthy way to deal with ideas, opinions, and needs. They become the benchmark for measuring the safety of the group. However, if the ground rules are broken, trust will be destroyed.

Periodically during the life of the group, the ground rules should be re-examined. Are they the best ones to meet the group's current needs? Are some rules more important than others? Have things changed since the last review?

Reviewing the ground rules reinforces behaviors and develops recommitment to the team and its purpose. At the beginning, rules are often created by the more vocal people in the group. If membership changes, the ground rules also need to change.

Openness and trust can be modeled and encouraged, but not legislated. These qualities are built in the moment-to-moment interactions that occur within the team. Effective partnerships allow each individual to bring his or her uniqueness to the situation and to use those strengths to create a more meaningful experience for everyone.

Share—Develop Common Understanding

Every interaction is co-created. Each person creates and is created by the current context. Each situation consists of many interdependent cause-and-effect relationships. There is a pattern of connectedness. Everything is related to everything else—one thing happens because other things have happened.

Because each moment is co-created, it is important to be able to separate your experience from another's by observing your own thoughts and perceptions. When you become aware of your internal state, you can choose your responses and direct your actions to influence those around you create an environment that fosters your dreams and values.

The following diagram shows the four-step process for creating a common understanding.

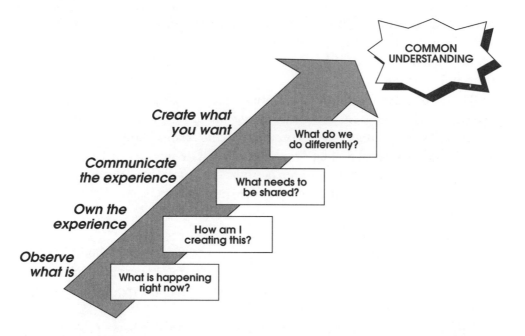

Observe What Is

Observation is the process whereby individuals identify what is occurring in the here and now. Observation is both internal—looking at my own attitudes, thoughts, feelings and ideas—and external—noticing what others are doing and saying, watching how they are interacting and sensing the prevailing mood or energy in the room. Observation involves being an active participant while simultaneously being detached enough to objectively note what is occurring in the external environment. It's a time of actively listening and observing to identify commonality of experience. When each member of the group utilizes his powers of observation, accountability, responsibility and communication are enhanced.

Own the Experience

Our beliefs, assumptions and expectations color our interpretations and observations of the moment. That is, we often blend our interpretations with our observations. For example, based on my experience and my internal perspective, I might interpret your rapid hand gestures as a sign of nervousness, regardless of whether you are feeling nervous. The key to being present in the moment is to identify the beliefs and assumptions that we bring with us and allow for other possible interpretations of others' words and actions.

To loosen up your powers of observation, ask yourself questions that uncover your preconceptions. What are my expectations for this interaction? What is important to me in this meeting? What am I predisposed to focus on? What do I want to occur? What do I think is possible or impossible? What am I afraid will happen?

The most powerful truth you can understand is that you create your own experience. When you believe that change comes from within yourself, you have the power to create the experiences you desire. You can consciously choose a new thought, belief or action. When team members deliberately choose their attitudes, beliefs, and actions, group interaction automatically becomes more genuine, which bolsters the quest for a common purpose.

Communicate the Experience

Synergistic partnerships are based on a shared understanding of the situation, yet rarely do two people interpret the same experience in the same way. Consequently, group members must share their perspectives with each other to develop a common focus.

This communication must distinguish between what is happening inside the individual you and what is occurring in the external environment. For communication to be effective, all parties must adhere to the following guidelines:

- Own your perceptions and actions. Take responsibility for your thoughts, feelings and actions by using the personal pronouns – I, me, my. Instead of saying "Life involves a learning process," say "I believe that life involves a learning process."

- Say what you see or hear. Describe the experience with sense statements: "I heard an irritating sound."

- Say what you think. Describe your thoughts and ideas: "I think it's possible to have both options."

- Describe what you are feeling in the moment: "I'm nervous about giving this speech." "I felt rejected when you didn't respond to my question."

- Say what you want. Describe your desires and intentions: "I want to explore other options before making a decision."

- Describe your actions in the moment: "I'm thinking about what you just said."

Create What You Want

This phase consists of seeing both sides of any issue and finding points in common. It's a process of bringing resources together to create an alliance of power and success. It's combining your resources in partnership to create a unique blending of different energies. Common ground results when group members are able to see all aspects of a situation as part of a bigger picture and bring together opposites to creatively solve the situation. Achieving a common perspective clears away confusion and allows for identification of the next step.

Create a Common Purpose

To effectively utilize the power pack of group dynamics, the team must develop a common purpose. In order to be truly "common," the shared purpose must be something that each person acknowledges as worthwhile and attainable. It must be beneficial to everyone involved and be of service to others.

Individuals will be energized by the belief that success can occur and that each person's talents can contribute to achieving the desired result. A well-formulated goal creates excitement and passion. This passion becomes the energy that enables the group to overcome obstacles, manage differences and develop synergistic action.

Concerning all acts of initiative and creation,
there is one elementary truth—
that the moment one definitely commits oneself,
the providence moves too.

—Johann Wolfgang von Goethe

*The first step…is the one
on which depend the rest.*

—Voltaire

*The impossible is possible
when people align with you.*

—Gita Bellin

Chapter 8

Turn On the Power

What gives a team a competitive advantage? Why does one group work more effectively than another? High-performing teams have a clearly defined purpose that sets the direction and becomes the focal point for energy alignment. This core purpose acts as a magnet to align daily behaviors and actions, to establish systems and processes, and to ensure intergroup alignment.

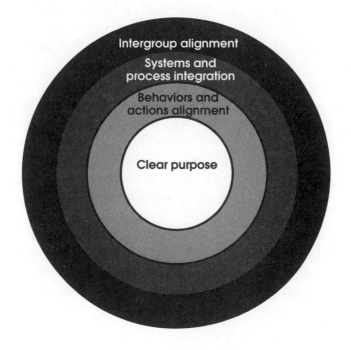

When energy is focused in a single direction, momentum is created and synergy develops. A clearly understood direction allows a team or organization to take advantage of opportunities, because the common focus naturally prioritizes decisions and actions.

For example, when Steve Jobs and Steve Wozniak created Apple Computer, they dreamed of changing the way people used computers. They envisioned individuals having personal computers that had the same capabilities as large mainframes. They focused their attention on creating a computer that anyone could use.

To do this, they created an innovative organizational environment that had no sense of boundaries or barriers. They hired young, brilliant, idealistic individuals who wanted to change the world. Jeans and T-shirts were normal attire, and it was not unusual for a team to work passionately through the night to develop a solution to a challenge. By holding onto a clear, strong vision, Apple created a computer that revolutionized the industry and set the stage for the information age.

Energy Alignment

Aligning the energy is a four-step process of clarifying the roles, behaviors, and direction of the team. Each step occurs through group discussion with input from all members. Each step is connected and lays the foundation for the next.

Clear purpose. This step consists of clarifying and developing a clear understanding of the team purpose by examining the question: What's important and why? This phase focuses on who we are as a team and what we should be doing.

Behaviors and actions. This step focuses on what has to happen in order to accomplish our agreed purpose. How are we going to work together? Time is spent identifying and agreeing to the behaviors that will be the group norms or standards.

Systems and processes. This step defines the tasks required to accomplish the purpose. It clarifies the roles and boundaries of how we will operate.

Intergroup alignment. This step identifies the interrelationships that affect accomplishment of task. It clarifies support needed in terms of resources and information.

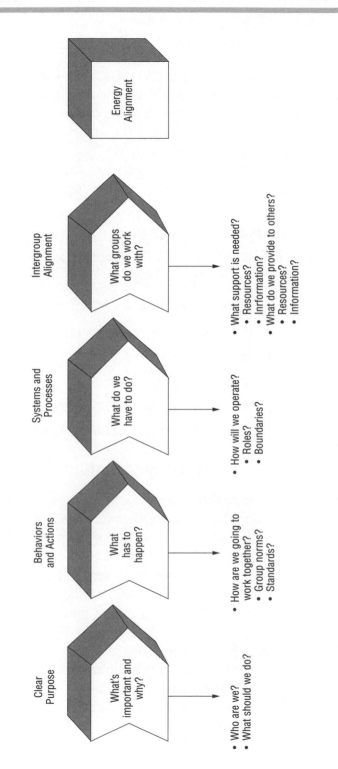

Clear Purpose

What's important and why?

- Who are we?
- What should we do?

Behaviors and Actions

What has to happen?

- How are we going to work together?
- Group norms?
- Standards?

Systems and Processes

What do we have to do?

- How will we operate?
- Roles?
- Boundaries?

Intergroup Alignment

What groups do we work with?

- What support is needed?
  - Resources?
  - Inrformation?
- What do we provide to others?
  - Resources?
  - Information?

Energy Alignment

Assess Your Current Energy

The first step to unleashing your team's collective energy is to understand how and where energy is being depleted. An unclear purpose will create ambiguity and confusion. Inconsistency between words and actions will decrease trust. Constricted processes will demotivate workers and energy will be wasted when boundaries are unclear.

To assess your group's level of energy, discuss with team members what your group is doing well and what requires improvement. Here are some questions you might ask:

- What is the purpose of our group?
- To what extent are our goals understood?
- Are any goals conflicting?
- What are the unique characteristics of our group?
- To what extent do we work together as a team?
- How effective are we in prioritizing and clarifying roles?
- Are all resources used effectively?
- Is there flexibility for individuality and input?
- How are differences or conflicts handled in our team?

Set the Environment

Once you have completed interviewing team members, analyze the information for patterns and themes that indicate challenges and areas of improvement. Use these themes for setting the environment for unleashing the power of commitment.

Start by providing a high-level summary of feedback to the group. Use this as a starting point for discussion about what makes an effective team. Realize that the word "team" means different things to different people. Each member of your group would describe a team in different terms, because their individual experiences frame their definitions.

Our mental patterns create the boundaries and limits to our world. When we enrich our internal perspectives, we create more options for how to perceive the same situation. Thus, the first step toward creating commitment is to set the environment and develop a common frame of reference that each member understands and accepts.

Setting the environment entails aligning different beliefs about teams and identifying the characteristics and behaviors required to create the team you want. Ask your group to answer the following key questions:

1. What are the characteristics of a team that I would want to join?

2. What does "partnership" mean? What would it look like in our group? How will I know it is a partnership?

3. What are the key strengths of our team?

4. What are the most important growth areas?

5. What are the benefits of membership?

Teamwork requires everyone's efforts
to flow in a single direction.

—Pat Riley

We are what and where we are
because we have first imagined it.

—Donald Curtis

Cherish your vision and your dreams
as they are the children of your soul.

—Napoleon Hill

Chapter 9

The Power of Commitment

Develop Ownership

Setting a team goal is the first step toward aligning the team's energy in a common direction. However, true power will not be released unless individual identification and ownership are created.

Ownership comes from understanding, accepting, and buying into the importance of the goal. Buy-in occurs when there is clarity and agreement on the tasks involved to achieve the goal. True ownership results from a process of communication whereby all team members can openly exchange information to clarify issues and discuss options. To be effective, this process must be based on genuine trust and openness, and both organizational and personal goals must be honestly addressed. The power of commitment is only released within the individual when the group's common purpose becomes personalized and internally accepted.

For this to happen, we must understand how the common purpose translates into action and how the tasks we perform relate to this purpose. We also need to see the group's mission as a concrete reflection of where the company is going; and actions by top management must be consistent with the stated purpose.

Create a Compelling Future

The future can be an incredibly exciting time of new direction and opportunity when we make the choice to embrace change and open ourselves to the experience. Focus and momentum are created by developing a group map or picture of the future. This picture identifies the factors that will impact the future and describes how the group desires and imagines the future will be.

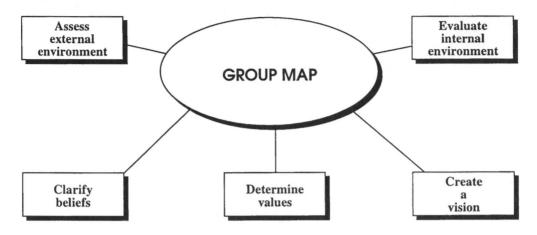

Creating a compelling future taps into emerging trends, identifies core values that provide direction on how to act, and describes the beliefs required to create what the group wants.

Assess the External Environment

This phase identifies the key components of the external environment that will change or affect the success of your team or organization. Discuss the following questions with your group:

- How are our customers' needs changing?
- What changes are occurring in the marketplace and what are our competitors doing?
- How will technology and government regulations change our business and industry?
- Where do we have a competitive advantage?
- What and where are the new opportunities for growth and expansion?

Evaluate the Internal Environment

The next phase looks at what you do and how well you do it. Discuss the following questions with your group:

- What are our strengths?
- What services do we provide and why?
- Why do our customers prefer our service?
- Where do we need to change?
- What could we do differently?

Create a Vision

Visions create a shared understanding of the present moment. They create a picture of a preferred future—placing boundaries on the unknown. A vision sets the direction for the group and explains where you are going and why.

Visions come from the heart. They create energy through passion and excitement for new possibilities. Visions describe our reason for being and sustain us through tough times. They provide a context larger than ourselves and set our expectations for what is possible. They act as a bridge between the present and the future.

A common vision binds people together around a set of ideals and creates an atmosphere of trust. A clearly defined vision sets a standard for coordinated activity. Without a common vision, individual needs take precedence over organizational needs.

Shared visions grow out individual visions. To align individual maps, a common context to the activity must be established. To be effective, a vision must focus on the long-term goals but be attainable through a series of short-term actions.

Establish an appropriate timeline for the next three years and visualize successful changes. Focus on what you want to create. Suspend your disbelief and create excitement by listening to each other's dreams. Discuss the following questions with your team.

- What would success look like?
- What would our business look like if it was the way we wanted it?
- What would be different?
- What would be our most important activities, services, or products?
- What systems would be in place?
- What would employees and managers do differently?

Establish the core purpose. Vision sets the direction, but action creates the result. Every vision must be translated into specific concrete behaviors and actions in order to achieve the goals.

Creating a vision is a process of re-examining and re-affirming the business you are in. It compels you to look at your business through a new looking glass and clarify your immediate goals. It identifies how your common purpose needs to change to incorporate the new vision and respond to changes in the environment.

Have your group consider the following questions?

- What business are we in and why? (Evaluate your products, services, customers and market niche.)

- What makes us different from our competitors?

- Why should we stay in this business? If our group did not exist, what critical results would be missing in the company?

- What knowledge, skills, and resources are available to develop new business?

- What do we need to do to be successful?

When we establish goals and clarify specific tasks through group discussion, the vision becomes personalized and ownership is created.

Determine Values

Commitment is the fuel that drives a vision. The power behind commitment is the congruency of beliefs and values. Values supply the context for our vision. By defining who we are and what we stand for, values bring our visions to life. Values demonstrate what we consider significant or hold in high esteem. They are the basic assumptions we make about ourselves. Our values describe a preferred outcome for our goals and are the standards by which decisions are made. Values of teamwork and participation, for example, establish the context for cooperation and collaboration.

Values provide a sense of direction for all employees and guidelines for day-to-day actions. Corporate values succeed only when employees can identify, embrace, and incorporate them into their daily work. Team values that ignore individual values will never succeed.

The first step in clarifying team values is for each team member to determine his own individual values by answering the following questions:

What is most important to me in my job? My career? Our team? Our business?

Next, discuss individual values to determine the key values for the group. Once an initial team list has been developed, go back to the team vision and ask: What values are needed to achieve this vision? Do any group values conflict with each other or the vision? Are any values more important than others to support our vision?

Refine the group's list as you examine the meaning of each value. Look at each value in relation to the others and describe each value by asking, "How will we know if this value is occurring?" Answer the question by describing the specific attitudes, actions, or feelings that would demonstrate the value.

Often this process will reveal that although we share the same values, we have attached different meanings to them. Our definitions set the boundaries to our experience. Although two people may both focus on the same value, they may feel unfulfilled and undervalued. For example, I might define "openness" as "sharing feelings" while your definition might focus on "communicating ideas." If you consistently communicate ideas without sharing your feelings, you will believe that you are being open, but I will likely be frustrated by your lack of sensitivity. Likewise, if I express openness by sharing my feelings, you may soon conclude that I am "too emotional" and that I never contribute new ideas. However, if the team clearly defines each key value, we will understand each other better. The process of defining group values is the first step in developing individual ownership of a standard set of behaviors.

Clarify Beliefs

Our beliefs are specific rules that govern our perception of reality. We see things according to what we believe. Our beliefs shape what we notice and color the way we look at things.

At the instant we experience a new moment, we attach meaning to it through our feelings, thoughts, reactions, and judgments. We assess each experience according to what we have noticed and we live each moment as if certain things are true.

The labels that we attach to each moment become our experience. Our reality is not shaped by events themselves, but by the meaning we attach to the experience. Our beliefs are generalizations based on our interpretations of past experiences. They describe our feelings about the event and color the present moment.

Every experience is an opportunity for us to become aware of and examine our beliefs. To change our experience requires a shift in our beliefs about what is possible. It requires a willingness to let go of what is not working and to focus on what we desire to create.

Take a few minutes now and list all the beliefs that limit you. For example:

- I'm not very smart.

- I don't have a college degree.

- My family was poor.

Now list all the beliefs that empower you to create the life you want. For example:

- I create my reality and I am responsible for what I create.

- Everything happens for a reason or purpose.

- Direction is more important than outcome.

Apply your lists to your team and organization. How do your disempowering beliefs affect your team experience and achievement of your vision?

Next, expand your personal list by adding any disempowering beliefs that stem from your work or team experience. For example:

- We don't have skilled people.

- Management doesn't support us.

- The union is always getting in our way.

- Teams are a waste of time, I could do it more quickly myself.

Now go back and reread your team's vision. What would you and the other members of your team need to believe in order to achieve your vision? Reframe your disempowering beliefs to allow for new possibilities. For example:

- Each person is important and contributes to the goal.

- Each person is unique and has special skills and talents to offer.

- We can accomplish our goals if we all work together.

Now, work with your team to create a list of beliefs necessary to accomplish your team's vision. Discuss how the beliefs affect your values, and make any adjustments necessary.

Merge Old into New

As a team defines its work and makes choices, boundaries are created that differentiate both the group and its individual members. At the group level, an identity emerges as a common purpose evolves. At the individual level, members focus on establishing a sense of belonging by evaluating each activity and identifying what it means for them.

Each boundary is an important part of the process of building a team. Each person is an individual with rights and needs. However, if the boundaries are rigid, separation results, which produces a psychological distance between individuals that must be bridged if the team is to accomplish something greater than its individual parts.

Each discussion of vision, values, and beliefs creates an opportunity to explore and expand our perceptions. By exploring for commonality, distances between individuals decrease and boundaries become blurred as new boundaries are agreed upon.

Change requires new behaviors, and new behaviors require new habits. New habits are developed through conditioning and reinforcement. Each time we take actions consistent with our vision and values, it becomes easier to take the next step. Remember, what we focus on, we will create.

Start today to develop daily rituals focused toward your goals. These rituals can be any activity, discussion, or question that reminds you of your vision and keeps you on track. For example:

- Display your vision, values and rules. Keep them on your desk and in your briefcase. Refer to them daily.

- Each day, ask yourself, "What actions can I take to stay on purpose?"

- Catch yourself doing something right. Acknowledge and reward yourself for progress and change of behavior.

- Review your values daily. Are any changes necessary?

- Start each meeting by choosing a value to emphasize.

- When discussions are off track, ask yourself, "How does this promote our vision?"

- Focus on solutions not problems. Ask yourself, "What can I learn from this? What could be good about this situation?"

- Review your vision daily. Enjoy each day and each step toward your goals. Record your feelings and reactions to the day in your progress journal.

Vision without action is just a dream.

—Joel Barker

You only grow by coming to the end of
something and by beginning something else.

—John Irving

Man's mind stretched to a new idea
never goes back to its original dimensions.

—Oliver Wendell Holmes

Chapter 10

The Power of Learning

The Art of Learning

Learning thrives in an atmosphere of exploration and discovery, but is hindered when people feel threatened. Learning occurs as a natural part of any work process when there is a willingness to improve and to use mistakes as steppingstones to awareness.

What is learning? It is an emotional process that creates change. This change can take many forms—a shift in ideas, thoughts, perceptions, understanding, or skills. Learning occurs when you

- develop self-awareness.

- see a situation differently.

- choose a different response.

- share your experience with others.

Develop self-awareness. Notice your thoughts, feelings, reactions, and intentions in the moment. Observe your interactions and identify your strengths and weaknesses. Develop your intuition and look beyond the rules— know when to apply them and when to let them go. Ask yourself, "What is my intention in this moment? What do I want to create?"

See a situation differently. Learning requires a change in your thinking and in your perception. Practice taking in new information that is relevant to your needs and interests and integrating it with current concepts or understanding. Develop a new skill or acquire new information that applies to your values, beliefs, or tasks.

Choose a different response. Each response, reaction, thought, or comment is a choice in the moment. Each new moment is an opportunity to translate your awareness into action and to link your action to specific goals. You can choose a different response by intending a different result or outcome than you have chosen before. Your intention sets the context for a new choice.

Share your experience with others. By sharing new understandings, ideas, and perceptions with others, our collective consciousness begins to change. Sharing your experience with a group converts tacit knowledge into explicit knowledge and creates an opportunity for individuals to change together through excitement and support. By clearly presenting information and our own point of view, and understanding other points of view, our dialogue creates a synergy that enables the collective knowledge to grow and expand. Effective dialogue requires a willingness to recognize and set aside personal assumptions and to openly examine another point of view.

In order to learn you must be willing to

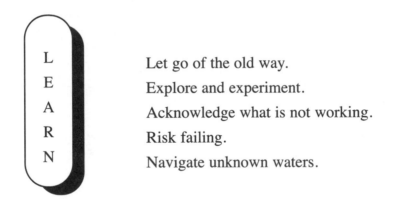

L — Let go of the old way.

E — Explore and experiment.

A — Acknowledge what is not working.

R — Risk failing.

N — Navigate unknown waters.

Let Go of the Old Way

Let go of your old beliefs, opinions, suppositions, expectations, and attachments. Open yourself to the moment and launch out beyond the known boundaries or accepted limitations. Look for patterns or links between activities and the accomplishment of goals.

Explore and Experiment

Develop an attitude of adventure and explore the unknown with the heart and mind of a beginner. Create an environment of emotional excitement. Be eager and curious to experience a new way. Examine new concepts. Encourage bold thinking and enjoy the process.

Acknowledge What Is Not Working

Grow through awareness of the world around you. Adapt to new realities by changing your attitudes, feelings, and energies. Assess and acknowledge what you know and don't know. Don't beat yourself up by getting down on the situation or yourself; instead, acknowledge what is happening and refocus your thoughts. Focus on your vision and then take action. When you acknowledge existing outcomes that are not what you desire, a new direction is defined.

Risk Failing

To succeed, you must first believe that success is possible. Use past successes as a catalyst for achievement in the present. Can you remember a time when you were anxious and concerned about something, only to have it work out? Focus on success and remember that a component of success is overcoming adversity. Recognize every obstacle as an opportunity to express more of yourself. Reinforce what you learn by keeping a record of your ideas, thoughts, and feelings throughout the process. See each result and outcome as valuable information that takes you one step closer to ultimate success.

Navigate Unknown Waters

Take one small step at a time. Build momentum and create a ripple effect by taking one step after another. Break the power of old conditioning, old values, and old beliefs and seek new perceptions and insights. Allow new ideas to emerge. Enjoy each moment and dare to succeed by focusing your energies toward your vision.

Turn Dreams into Reality

Each of the above steps create the foundation for turning dreams into reality. In order to pioneer a new way or discover new frontiers—whether in science, medical research, or technology advancement—we must be willing to move beyond the known boundaries of today. "To go where no one has gone before" requires courage and commitment to a new way.

Old beliefs about gravity, about traveling faster than the speed of sound, and about surviving in outer space had to be set aside in order for mankind to travel into space and reach for the moon—and beyond. It was necessary to explore and experiment beyond the comfort zone of present knowledge—to experiment with rocket combustion chambers, multistage rockets and unmanned space flights—and each phase of space required the courage to acknowledge what didn't work, as well as what did work. When booster rockets failed or other plans were shown to be invalid, systems had to be redesigned and beliefs and concepts had to be examined and challenged.

Each of these steps required a willingness to risk failing and to learn from mistakes, even at the cost of lives. Each astronaut was willing to put his life on the line because he believed that the mission was more important than any one individual.

Because man had never before traveled into outer space, every step required navigating unknown waters. When Neil Armstrong stepped onto the moon and said, "That's one small step for man, one giant leap for mankind," he acknowledged the effort, commitment, and courage that each person must expend in order to go beyond the boundaries of today and navigate unknown waters.

Set the Team Environment

A team learning environment is created by establishing the following climate:

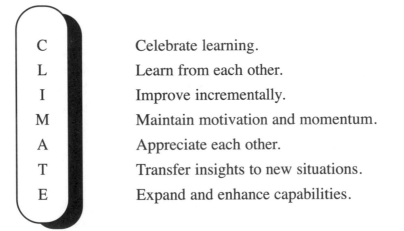

C	Celebrate learning.
L	Learn from each other.
I	Improve incrementally.
M	Maintain motivation and momentum.
A	Appreciate each other.
T	Transfer insights to new situations.
E	Expand and enhance capabilities.

Celebrate Learning

Create a cultural mind-set of cooperation and open communication where team members feel free to speak about what they have learned. Encourage individuals to be self-directed learners who view mistakes as opportunities for growth and understanding. Challenge beliefs that restrict learning (for example, "No pain, no gain"), and replace them with beliefs that empower the individual to pursue progress ("Elicit effortless energy," for example). Create daily opportunities to explore and share insights and new ideas.

Support this process with experiential learning labs to explore new ways of thinking and behaving. In these structured learning experiences, you learn about yourself and your self in relation to others through a series of group exercises, interactions, and individual reflection. The focus is on developing self-awareness and shifting from "automatic pilot" reactions and patterns of living to consciously choosing the life you want to live.

Learn From Each Other

Value differences in learning styles and perceptions within the group. Encourage discussion of differing viewpoints for the purpose of understanding possible new perspectives. Listen to one another and suspend disbelief in order to truly hear. Explore differences in perception for insights that can create a foundation for new growth. Conduct "lessons learned" sessions to create new, innovative processes.

Lessons learned sessions are meetings designed specifically to share stories and learning experiences by discussing a variety of viewpoints and participants' insights. The purpose is to gain a new perspective and shift the group's collective knowledge or consciousness by identifying and bringing to the surface mental models and assumptions that affect the situation. These sessions can be incorporated into daily work meetings or set up as special gatherings focused on specific new projects.

Improve Incrementally

Successful teams acknowledge that progressive learning is built on experience, one step at a time. Learning occurs through individual steps rather than one large leap and each new insight creates the foundation for the next discovery.

The Japanese describe this process as *kaizen*, or continuous improvement. Kaizen occurs through a gradual and constant change of standards, resulting in ongoing improvement that involves everyone. Kaizen assumes that our way of life deserves to improve continually and that improvement must be standardized across the organization. Each improvement then creates the next step for change.

Maintain Motivation and Momentum

Learning becomes an easy part of the daily process when individuals can attach personal significance to an activity or insight. To enhance team-wide understanding, focus shared insights on specific processes or activities that support short or long-term goals. Create an understanding of new concepts by connecting the information to something familiar or already known. Start with specific, concrete examples and then expand to more complex or abstract concepts. Demonstrate possible practical uses for new information and challenge any assumptions that would limit the perception and usefulness of the insights.

Appreciate Each Other

Take time to reflect on and appreciate the strengths of each member of your team. Think about each person and ask, "What would I miss if this person was not part of our team?" Record in your progress journal the qualities of each person. Add to your list when you notice other positive qualities emerging.

Shine the spotlight on yourself and ask, "What qualities do I bring to the job that others value?" Record these in a list and compare your strengths with the strengths of others on the team. Notice the balance between complementary skills as well as areas that need improvement.

Create a process for feedback and appreciation through a special time of giving of gifts. Allow each member the opportunity to give and receive the gift of appreciation. Have each person complete the statement, "I enjoy working with you because…" or "I'm glad you're part of our team because…" or "What I value and appreciate in you is…" Focusing your mind on the positive qualities of another person automatically shifts your disposition toward affirmation and appreciation.

Transfer Insights to New Situations

The real power of learning is the ability to translate insights into actions and apply them to daily activities. Before implementing a new idea in a crucial situation, create opportunities to try out new behaviors and new thinking. Take time to compare perceptions to reality; role-play, practice new skills and make adjustments. The greater the change, the greater the need for a time to adapt, assimilate and gain confidence in new behaviors. Specific time for assimilation must be built into implementation plans and day-to-day operations if learning is to be effective.

Support implementation with action learning. Learning by doing is a process whereby a project team is assigned a real business issue and asked to solve the issue and record lessons learned in the process. The procedure focuses on framing the situation in a new way, gathering data, integrating findings, and putting recommendations into action. Learning is supported through coaching and personal feedback, as well as reflection, inquiring, and self-awareness activities.

Expand and Enhance Capabilities

When we make the choice to focus our daily activities on expanding and growing, we experience the power and joy of learning. We can act as living examples of how we want the organization to operate by building in time during our daily activities for reflection, questioning, observation, and sharing information and ideas.

Here are some daily activities you can use to create a learning atmosphere and mind-set:

- Start each day by asking yourself, "What is important for me to learn today?" or "What do I need to focus my attention on?"

- Before meetings, take a moment to reflect, and ask yourself, "What do I know about this situation? What facts or information do I need to clarify or explore further? Do I need more information before taking action?"

- As you work on an activity during the day, stop and ask yourself, "What is good about this situation? Why is it important? What can I learn from this?"

- During meetings, take a moment to observe and value the differences within the group. Notice who is actively engaged in the process and what each person brings to the discussion.

- Throughout the meeting, become aware of different thought patterns. Notice when the group is searching, exploring, and questioning multiple factors of a situation. Then observe when the discussion converges into a narrow field or focus. Use these observations as signals for further discussion. You may need to go with the flow or change the direction to create a new focus or paradigm.

- Throughout the day, challenge your assumptions about what you know of a situation. Explore new options.

- Remind yourself of opportunities to learn. Post the question, "What can I learn from this?" on your wall or in your daily planner. Each time you see the question during the day, take a moment to answer it.

- At the end of each day, record four or five key insights in your progress journal. Record new ideas, your successes, and the lessons you learned.

Use these snapshots from the past to create the future by sharing key lessons learned with other team members and exploring new ways to interact.

The life which is not examined is not worth living.

—Plato

Everything starts as a seed idea.

—Raymond Charles Barker

*Creating is the place where the human spirit
shines its brightest light.*

—Robert Fritz

Chapter 11

The Power of Creativity

Power of Ideas

To ignite creativity within ourselves and our groups, we must first understand how our minds process information. The brain categorizes ideas by association, creating a network of related concepts. It automatically organizes new material by grouping ideas and words together. Our minds function by linking ideas together in a sequential pattern—a logical order of arrangement based on linear, time/space, association, or imagery progression.

When information enters our minds, our brains automatically correct and complete the information and link it to other patterns. Creativity occurs when we make new connections and thereby create new patterns. The more memory associations we can form, the easier it is to remember previous information and create new connections. Everyone possesses creative ability, and we can learn to tap into and enhance this valuable resource. Creative people have refined the process of establishing multiple links for new ideas and concepts.

During the 1960s, researchers studied the differences between the brain's left and right hemispheres. They identified that the two hemispheres have different but overlapping skills and ways of processing information. Each is dominant in certain activities.

Left brain	*Right brain*
words/language	forms or patterns
logic	images and pictures
sequence	spatial awareness
linear	holistic (big picture)
analysis of details	imagination
concrete	intuition

We use both sides of our brains, but we tend to prefer one side or the other. The ratio of left brain/right brain preference that each of us utilizes affects how we process information, approach our work, and live our lives. Creativity results from the interaction between both sides of the brain. To be more creative requires that we move from our preferred dominance to explore possibilities in a new way.

You can begin to identify your preferences right now by taking this little test: When confronted with a new challenge, do you first look for a logical sequence (left brain), or do you immediately become aware of your intuitive gut reaction (right brain)? When you see a new piece of machinery for the first time, do you immediately wonder how it works (left) or do you take a step back and admire the motion, sounds, and size (right)? When you listen to an elaborate story, do you find yourself muttering, "Get to the point" (left), or is your mind awash in the visual imagery that the storyteller evokes (right)? If you have a balanced left brain/right brain relationship, you might find that your mind shifts quickly from reveling in imagination to focusing on and analyzing a specific detail within your mental picture. Even if one hemisphere has clear dominance, over time you can "reformat" your brain to draw on elements from the subordinate hemisphere by consciously choosing to adopt a new perspective. Explore new options by playing with non-dominant traits. Notice how you feel and observe how your mind begins to create new connections. Use the following ideas to start shifting from left brain thinking to right brain thinking, or vice versa.

Left to Right	*Right to Left*
• Look for the big picture of connections.	• Take notes and set priorities.
• Explore irrelevant information.	• Develop goals and timelines.
• Respond to body language.	• Practice activity or process.
• Change your physiology. Move, stand up, or walk.	• Outline or list facts and information.
• Doodle or draw a picture of the situation.	• Break activity into specific components.
• Close your eyes and visualize what you want.	• Gather more detailed information.
• Become aware of surrounding colors, sounds, aromas.	• Evaluate and eliminate information.

Memory. The foundation of creativity flows from our ability to access information from within and make new associations. Memory is anchored in our minds and bodies by:

- Repetition—the reoccurrence of an event or information that creates a habitual pattern.

- Association—the linkage of a particular meaning to information already established in our memories.

- Intensity—the level of emotional impact of a thought or activity.

- Involvement—the number of senses activated and linked to the event.

Memories are activated by triggers of association. The meaning, words, or pictures linked to the memory trigger other associations. Have you ever smelled fresh bread or a pie baking and found yourself thinking about your mother's homemade desserts? Have you ever heard a song and remembered your first date or a special occasion? Have you ever watched snow falling and remembered a childhood Christmas?

Each of the above memories acted as a key to release other memories. This same process of association produces creativity whenever knowledge is unlocked and re-examined in ways that create new associations. To facilitate creativity, we must establish a conducive environment for effectively triggering associations. Observe your team interactions and one-on-one communications. Does the structure of your meetings encourage breakthrough thinking. Do team members feel "safe" approaching an issue through the back door? Is adequate time devoted to exploring new ideas and approaches to problem solving and planning? Are you so intent on "getting to the point" or "sticking to the agenda" that you miss the color, texture or aroma of the discussion? Or are you too busy daydreaming about your "next great idea" to focus on the step-by-step implementation process of the current idea being discussed?

Breakthrough Thinking

Breakthrough thinking occurs when someone connects information or ideas in ways that alter the status quo. To shift a paradigm requires courage and the willingness to see a situation differently. It's accepting the risk of looking foolish and stepping beyond your fear into the uncomfortable realm of the unknown.

Jim McCann describes himself as an "entrepreneurial voyeur" who is constantly seeking new strategies and techniques to grow his company. Back in 1987, everyone viewed the retail flower business as mom-and-pop shops where customers came to buy flowers.

McCann broke the rules of the game and blew away old assumptions to create a huge new business—flowers by phone. He established the first national flower-selling telephone service by promoting flowers as gifts through an easy order system of 24-hour toll-free telephone service. By the end of the first year, his 1-800-FLOWERS number had created sales of over $500,000.

He focused on getting customers accustomed to buying gifts over the phone and developing reliable relationships so the customers would come back. By 1996 his telecenters had annual sales of over $250 million, with flowers as part of gift baskets and retail sales.

When you are willing to embrace uncertainty and ambiguity, release your stranglehold on irrelevant worries, and learn from your mistakes, you are ready for breakthrough thinking.

To establish an environment where new associations can be triggered, information can be reframed or seen in new ways, and ideas can be chunked or grouped differently, create the following conditions:

- Respect individuals (and individuality). Recognize that no two people solve a problem or look at a situation in the same way, and celebrate this diversity as a strength rather than viewing it as an impediment to the process.

- Encourage bold thinking. Protect new ideas from ridicule. Listen to and explore each new idea.

- Develop creativity through practice. Reframe ideas and hook them into new patterns to create a fresh perspective.

- Encourage and develop intuition. Take meaningful and intelligent risks.

- Put ideas into action. Recognize mistakes as opportunities for learning. Continually ask, "What can we learn from this?"

- Encourage individuals to become resources for each other. Make asking for help and relying on the experience of others part of your routine. Acknowledge individual strengths and celebrate interactive participation.

Developing Creativity

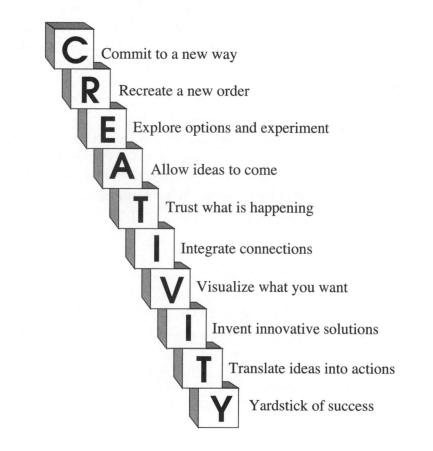

C — Commit to a new way

R — Recreate a new order

E — Explore options and experiment

A — Allow ideas to come

T — Trust what is happening

I — Integrate connections

V — Visualize what you want

I — Invent innovative solutions

T — Translate ideas into actions

Y — Yardstick of success

Commit to a New Way

Creativity is a choice. When we decide to see a situation differently by consciously clarifying and challenging our attitudes and actions, we create a new focus. Creativity occurs in many different ways—one idea leads into another, and soon a winning idea is born.

Robert Plath, a former Northwest Orient Airline pilot, was tired of lugging 40 pounds of manuals with him on each flight, so he attached a cart onto his carry-on bag. His fellow pilots laughed at his suitcase on wheels, but today his invention—a rolling suitcase with wheels and a retractable handle— can be seen in any airport worldwide.

In 1989 Plath created a prototype mold for his suitcase by using a household vacuum cleaner and a stove. He sent the molds to Asia to be manu-factured and started selling his Rolloboards by mail order to airline colleagues. By 1992, he had sold over $14 million worth of suitcases through distributors, and by 1994 had created over $30 million in sales—all from a simple idea.

We "assume" when we unquestionably believe that something is true. Analyzing our assumptions means moving beyond the fixed boundaries of our present paradigms and changing the limitations that we place on ourselves. Creativity is released when we change the fundamental rules of a situation. We can start by looking at how the problem is defined. Ask, "What is creating this situation?" and "What are we presuming to be true?"

List all the assumptions that would have to be true in order for us to see the situation the way that we do. Examine the list to determine which assump-tions are most critical to support our viewpoint. Next, explore the impact of changing these key assumptions. Ask, "What would happen if…?" Take note of the beliefs that surface and get in the way of the desired outcome.

Recreate a New Order

To foster creativity, recombine ideas, information, assumptions, and beliefs into a new order. Consciously and deliberately reconnect the compo-nents into a new sequence that produces a new way of thinking or acting. Exercise courage to unhook prejudices and let go of old ideas to generate new ones.

Kindle the fire of new ideas by borrowing and applying information from other fields. Focus on improvement by asking, "Where is the hidden opportu-nity in this situation? How can this [fill in the blank] be made to work better? Which needs are not being met and which customers are not satisfied?"

Look for and expect new insights. A new paradigm forces us to look in a new direction. When we are willing to challenge our basic assumptions and construct new models of reality, we will notice things we have never seen before.

For example, Albert Einstein developed his theory of relativity by shifting his paradigm about time, space, and matter by asking questions. One day, as he sat reflecting on the speed of light, he asked himself the question, "What would it be like to ride on the end of a light beam?" As he imagined moving at the speed of light, he thought about what he would see if he looked at a clock. He realized that because he would be traveling at the same speed as the image of the clock hands moving, time would appear to stand still. This breakthrough concept led to his theory that time and space are only concepts created from our sensory perceptions.

Experiment and Explore Options

Link new information to specific actions to accomplish your goals. Think of yourself as an artist weaving together options and alternatives. Be willing to experiment and learn from new experiences. Explore how change in one area creates change in another area. For example, notice how the type and sequence of information changes when you shift your goals.

Develop a hypothetical "what if" scenario and explore the range of possibilities. Describe probable future situations and factors—both internal and external—that could affect successful completion of your goals. Build alternative action scenarios and use this information to guide and direct your decisions.

When Bill Gates and Paul Allen founded Microsoft, they saw the potential of Intel's 8080 microprocessor to make computers affordable for everyone. They asked the question, "What would happen if computing was nearly free?" Their answer was that computers would be everywhere and that the future was in developing new applications and software to meet the demand. By anticipating the future, they created a multi-billion dollar company.

Allow Ideas to Flow

We all possess an infinite source of ideas, but many of us have learned to channel our creativity into narrow, predictable bottles. We can pop the cork on new ideas by reformulating questions, asking for more than one answer or probing for increased clarity. When we suspend judgment on whether or not a specific concept will work, and simply record all information, we allow new ideas to surface.

As group members suggest new perspectives, bring together possibilities and spin-offs through free association. Combine, integrate, and synthesize experiences to create new patterns. See every situation as an opportunity to learn and to generate new ideas. Notice areas of change and areas of new learning and be open to new possibilities.

When we are committed to finding new ways and are open to exploring our thoughts, innovative ideas for products and services emerge easily. The climate of creativity at 3M led to the development of Post-It notes from an employee's experiments with an unsuccessful batch of glue. American Airlines unexpectedly increased its market share significantly after installing the Sabre reservations system. They created the system to make it easier and faster for travel agents to write tickets, but because the system was designed to list American flights first, travel agents tended to book flights on American more often.

Trust the Process

Set aside your perfect pictures of what "should" be happening and observe what is unfolding in the present moment. Awaken yourself to the experience—your thoughts, feelings and emotions. Maintain a flow of ideas through processes such as brainstorming and mind mapping. Shelter new ideas from criticism and judgment. Take time to allow ideas to percolate.

Integrate Connections

Interpret the meaning of new insights. Develop an awareness of associations and interconnectedness. Identify multiple effects—change causing change. Listen to and trust your inner voice. Let your intuitive responses guide your actions. Use your inner senses to highlight areas of emphasis and to direct your next steps.

Visualize the Desired Outcome

Apply new insights to your existing vision. Redefine areas that need to change. Visualize a clear, refined image of the desired outcome. Notice any new thoughts, assumptions, or emotions that emerge during this process. Take steps to counteract any limiting thoughts. Pop the cork on new ideas, then focus on the process by asking, "What needs to happen to produce…?" Engage your feelings and other senses in your visualization.

Walt Disney dreamed about a theme park where families could be together and enjoy a unique, fun experience. He saw clearly in his mind how every piece worked together to create the story—the fantasy. He saw how each expression, reaction, and action created the personalities and characters that would be appealing to his audience. Many people told him it wouldn't work—that people would not pay to live a fantasy. But today the company he created provides unique experiences worldwide through its theme parks and movies.

Invent Innovative Solutions

Anticipate the future by stepping back and looking at the situation strategically. Look at the big picture and identify trends that could impact your plans. Extrapolate these trends into the future and envision a solution.

Avoid premature closure or rejection of an idea. Remain open to the possibility that your idea is feasible. Examine options by asking, "Why would this work? What would be needed to implement? Has this been tried before? Did it work? Why or why not?"

Review your vision and take note of your intuitive feelings or gut reaction to the effectiveness of the solution. Next, ask yourself, "What information do I need in order to determine whether or not this idea is feasible? How do I obtain this information?"

Translate Ideas into Action

Write out your ideas in detail. State your assumptions by looking at what is behind the idea and consider other ideas that need to be explored. List questions that need to be answered before you can proceed. Obtain the necessary information and solicit feedback from the people most affected by the situation.

Develop a detailed action plan that includes the following steps:

1. Visualize success. Look at the situation as if you were an impartial observer. Visualize the proposed changes occurring. Identify boundaries such as time, skills and resources. Focus on internal and external linkages. Notice elements that will differ from your present circumstances—new alliances, products, or services.

2. Develop a detailed plan. Identify specific action steps according to a time line. Identify indicators of success. Establish checkpoints. Determine operational issues and identify new opportunities.

3. Monitor progress. Review, prioritize, and assess opportunities for improvement. Identify risks and likelihood of success.

Yardstick of Success

In today's turbulent business environment, creativity is one of the most important keys to developing a competitive advantage. Creativity allows organizations to enter new markets quicker, respond more effectively to changing customer needs, and regain eroded customer confidence. It increases flexibility in processes and creates opportunities to lower costs and enhance productivity.

Innovative companies develop processes and incentives for developing creative solutions. For example, 3M has a policy stating that 30 percent of division's sales must come from products that didn't exist four years ago. Each division has a great deal of latitude to allocate funds as they wish, but a project must show a profit within two years or be terminated.

Anyone at 3M can propose a new project. The 30 percent rule creates a situation where all managers are looking for new products—so if an engineer approaches his manager with a new idea and it is rejected, he often goes to another department head to find support.

To encourage individual initiative, 3M operates from the premise that no market or product is too small. When an idea is accepted, a new venture team is formed of volunteers from different disciplines who can return to their home division if the project fails—in a sense, these teams consist of "true believers" focused on the idea.

Tools and Techniques

Promoting new ideas and creative thinking can be facilitated by the use of tools and techniques that help to break down the usual barriers to change, such as resistance to new ideas, snap judgments, criticism, negative thought patterns, and loss of focus. Several techniques that work particularly well in group settings are brainstorming, mind mapping, cause-and-effect analysis, affinity, and relationship diagrams.

Brainstorming

Brainstorming is an idea-generating technique used to help a group unlock as many ideas as possible in a short time. It helps to document what a team knows, stimulates team creativity by building on the ideas of others, and gets everyone involved.

To brainstorm effectively, you must defer judgment or evaluation of ideas, and create a freewheeling atmosphere in which each person voices whatever ideas come to mind. Participants are encouraged to hitchhike on the ideas of others, and every idea is written down, regardless of its apparent quality. The rules for brainstorming:

- State the purpose clearly.
- Offer one idea at a time.
- Don't criticize or evaluate ideas.
- Don't discuss ideas as they are suggested. Simply write them down and keep the process moving.
- Build on others' ideas.
- Record all ideas.

It is important to suspend judgment and discussion of ideas until the brainstorming process has been exhausted. Some of the best ideas come late in the process, often as the result of "hare-brained" suggestions that might otherwise not be considered. The magic of brainstorming lies in its no-holds-barred ability to elicit imaginative solutions.

Once all ideas have been suggested and recorded, the group may prioritize ideas and choose to focus on those with the greatest merit. Further discussion may clarify ideas and suggest ways to refine and implement the best ideas. During the discussion phase, previously discarded ideas may be reincorporated or used as catalysts to propel the discussion forward.

Mind Mapping

Mind mapping is a brainstorming tool that helps the group organize its thoughts and make new connections between thoughts and ideas. A mind map consists of the following items:

- A central image or graphic represents of the problem or information being mapped.

- Ideas flow freely from the central image through brainstorming.

- Each idea is represented by key words.

- Key words are connected to the central focus with lines.

- Colors, symbols, and images are used to highlight ideas and connections.

    Every mind map is a unique product of the person or team that produces it.

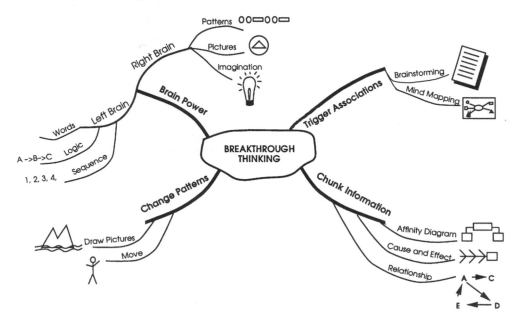

    The rules for mind mapping:

- Let ideas flow from the center image.

- Use nouns and verbs for key words.

- Print key words on lines.

- Use size of print, line, or image to depict emphasis.

- Use arrows and colors to connect ideas.

Cause-and-effect Analysis

The cause-and-effect diagram is a tool to help analyze problems. It uses lines and symbols to represent the relationships between effects and their causes. Cause-and-effect analysis helps a group reach a common understanding of a problem while clarifying gaps in existing knowledge.

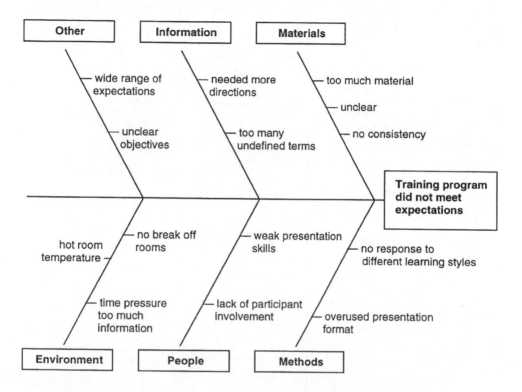

In order to create a cause and effect diagram follow these steps:

1. Agree on a statement that describes the selected problem in terms of what it is, and where and when it occurs.

2. Place the problem statement in a box on the right side of your diagram and draw an arrow leading to it.

3. Define the major categories of possible causes and label the branches.

4. Brainstorm possible causes for each category by asking "Why does it happen?"

5. When the diagram is completed, circle root causes and prioritize. Verify the impact of each cause by gathering data. Brainstorm possible solutions.

Affinity Diagram

An affinity diagram is a visual representation of ideas grouped by subject. It is most often used for complex, difficult problems where a large number of diverse ideas have been generated. The purpose of an affinity diagram is to allow the group to organize in a meaningful way ideas generated in a brainstorming session, and to encourage new creative breakthroughs in the way individuals think about an issue.

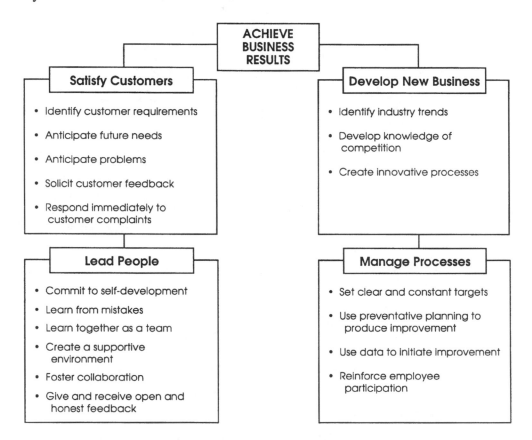

Follow these steps to construct an affinity diagram:

1. Collect data on topic (often through brainstorming).

2. Transfer information onto cards or Post-Its.

3. Examine the ideas for possible groupings.

4. Diagram the groups, showing the relationships between groups.

5. Title and label the diagram.

Relationship Diagram

A relationship diagram is a visual map of cause-and-effect relationships in a complex issue. It shows the direction and strength of these relationships and is useful for identifying and analyzing root causes. A relationship diagram can be used on its own by identifying the problem and brainstorming possible causes, or it can be used in conjunction with a cause-and-effect diagram.

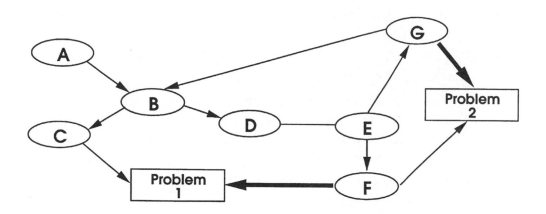

Follow these steps to construct a relationship diagram:

1. Identify the main problem.

2. Brainstorm related issues or potential causes.

3. Draw diagram by using connecting arrows to depict direction and strength of relationships.

4. Identify data that supports the assumptions and identify additional data requirements.

5. Determine appropriate action steps.

Team Creativity

The foundation of team creativity is an environment that stimulates breakthrough thinking by utilizing techniques and methods that complement and leverage the workings of the brain, triggering associations and reframing information.

To establish a creative environment, focus on these goals:

- Balancing activities between left and right brain processes.

- Generating ideas by association. Use processes like brainstorming or mind mapping.

- Chunking information into groups. Use affinity, cause-and-effect, or relationship diagrams.

- Reframing stated problems or situations. Use an inside-out approach to explore issues by reversing the characteristics or turning the facts upside down. For example, instead of having your company design the product, ask your customers to design it.

- Reversing daily thinking patterns. Change your physiology through movement or drawing.

Facilitation is like having a quiver of arrows and pulling out the right one at the right time. Successful facilitation occurs when the right tool is used for the right situation. The key is to determine which method best matches the need. Sometimes, the best facilitation is to use a combination of methods to create the desired outcome.

For example, a division vice president of a large pharmaceutical company asked me to facilitate a vision-development session with his key division managers. These managers had spent three days at a strategic planning retreat and had worked on a vision statement but could not agree on a vision.

I knew that I needed to change the group's thinking patterns from left brain "wordsmithing" to right brain "big picture" intuitive thinking. I also knew it was important to incorporate the work they had already done without getting stuck in previous thought patterns. To do this I designed the session to be a combination of activities. Within two hours, the group agreed on a vision and identified key steps for implementation.

The following activities outline the strategy I used to help the group move from left brain to right brain thinking. You can use the same process in your group or organization.

Pattern Changing Activity (5 minutes)

1. Use your non-dominant hand to write on a blank piece of paper the top four issues facing your company.

2. Look at your list and identify the most critical issue. Now turn over the page and continue to use your non-dominant hand to write down this issue. Try to write it as large as possible.

3. Now write on a new page why you think the issue you have selected is the most critical. Write as small as possible.

Discussing Issues and Observations (10 minutes).

Discuss with the group:

- What issues did you list?

- Which are the most critical, and why?

- Was it easy or difficult to write with your opposite hand?

- What did you notice during the process?

Change Thinking Patterns by Changing Physiology (5 minutes)

Discuss confident and non-confident physiology with the group:

Non-confident: When you're feeling unsure of yourself, how do you walk? How do you breathe? In which direction are your eyes focused? Other characteristics? (Do you walk slowly, have shallow breath, are your eyes downcast?)

Confident: When you're feeling confident, how do you walk? How do you breathe? Where do you focus your eyes? Other characteristics? (Do you have a solid steady walk, take deep breaths, keep your eyes straight ahead, swing your arms?)

Change physiology: Walk around the room clockwise feeling confident, knowing your purpose and sense of direction, and feeling totally sure of your skills.

Generate Ideas by Association (30 minutes)

Develop three vision mind maps (Industry, Organization, Division):

- As you walk around the room, think about three years from now. How will things be different? (A lot of successes have happened. What systems are in place? What are the most important activities?)

- Take a pen and write on the first mind map changes in your industry.
- Walk around the room again, stopping to add more information to your map.
- Walk around the room again and identify changes to your organization and to the division.
- Add these ideas to the second and third maps.

Chunk Information (20 minutes)

Categorize information on your three mind maps:

- Look at each mind map and identify patterns.
- Use an affinity diagram to group changes and effects.

Develop a Big Picture of the Future (50 minutes)

Develop a vision statement based on the information and ideas generated in each of the preceding steps.

- What is our purpose?
- What do we need to do to be successful?
- What makes us different from our competitors?

Determine next steps

- List issues and barriers to success.
- Prioritize issues.
- Identify next steps.

Whatever you can do or dream,
you can begin it.

—Johann Wolfgang von Goethe

Opportunity now lies,
not with perfecting routines,
but with taking advantage of instability.

—Tom Peters

The ability to influence reality
comes from seeing structures
that are controlling behavior and events.

—Peter M. Senge

Chapter 12

The Power of Leverage

Build a Competitive Advantage

In order to be competitive in today's fast-paced global markets, an organization must be able to attract and retain customers by establishing a product or service that is perceived as unique. Perceived value is established by the interaction of three key factors: cost, quality, and benefit.

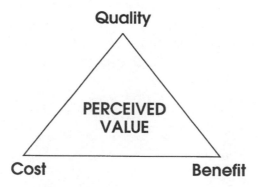

How much weight will be assigned to each of the three factors depends on the buyer. For one customer, price might be the deciding factor. For another, as long as the price is in a competitive range, quality or perceived benefit might determine their choice.

To achieve a competitive advantage, a firm must make a choice about the advantage it seeks to attain. For example, if a company sets out to be the low-cost provider in its industry, it must find and exploit all sources of cost advantage, such as economies of scale, technological advances, and readily available raw materials. Typically, a low-cost provider sells a standard, no-frills product and achieves profitability through low overhead.

Another strategy is to create a lower-priced version of a premium-quality product. Rather than attempting to be the overall low-cost leader, a company might choose to be the low-cost provider in a specific niche within the market. For example, Toyota designed the Lexus to compete with Mercedes and BMW at the high end of the luxury car market. By creating a luxury quality vehicle at a lower price than its high-end competitors, Lexus was able to capture significant market share quickly.

A company that depends heavily on a price advantage to sustain its market share runs the risk of being undercut by a lower-cost supplier. Companies that create perceived value through quality or benefit are more likely to develop a sustainable competitive advantage, because it is more difficult for a competitor to establish a reputation for superior quality or benefit than it is to simply cut prices.

A firm that seeks to be unique through quality or service maintains its profits by charging a premium price for that perceived value. For this strategy to work, the firm must truly be unique or be perceived as unique by its customers. To create a unique niche, the company must fully understand its customers' needs and be able to translate those needs into new products or services. Peter Drucker says, "Quality in a product or service is not what the supplier puts in. It is what the customer is willing to pay for.... Customers pay only for what is of use to them and gives them value."

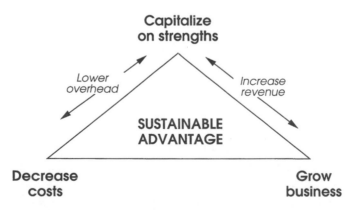

Create a sustainable advantage. To create a sustainable advantage, a company must decrease its costs, capitalize on its strengths, and develop ways and opportunities to grow its business.

Although each of these is important for survivability, most companies have focused their attention on decreasing costs through such strategies as total quality management, process improvement, and restructuring. Generally, even when processes have been re-engineered, businesses overlook opportunities to create an advantage through capitalizing on their strengths or growing the business, because the power of leverage has not been used effectively.

Understanding Leverage

Creating leverage is the process of translating a group's unique skills and abilities into a distinctive basis of differentiation that enables you to capitalize on your strengths and grow your business. Whereas cost-based strategies focus on external models of change, leverage facilitates and maximizes the impact of internal changes and harnesses the power of commitment, learning, and creativity.

Use the following guidelines to create leverage within your organization:

- *Build on something you already have*. Use your strengths—your skills, technology, processes, customer base, information databases—as a springboard for new products, services, and capabilities.

- *Develop a leverage mind-set*. Open yourself to new possibilities by recognizing that there are multiple ways to do something—there is no right or wrong way. Be willing to step outside the box of tradition and "the way it's always been done" and reinvent the rules of the game.

- *Implement multiple-impact strategies*. Uncover and seek to understand the interconnectedness of your systems, products, and services and look for opportunities to create an exponential increase that is greater than the sum of its parts. For examples, most businesses sell their basic product but make no effort to sell their customers anything else. If related products and services can be developed, these back-end sales are usually more profitable, because you don't have to pay twice to find the customer.

- *Value differences and take advantage of them*. Your strengths can complement another's weakness. For example, you could set up noncompetitive and synergistic joint ventures with other companies and access each other's customer base. An exclusive fashion store could sell to the customers of a specialty shoe store.

Creating Leverage

Leverage can be illustrated as a dynamic upward force, where each stage provides a foundation for the next level and each successive level builds on the energy of the preceding stage.

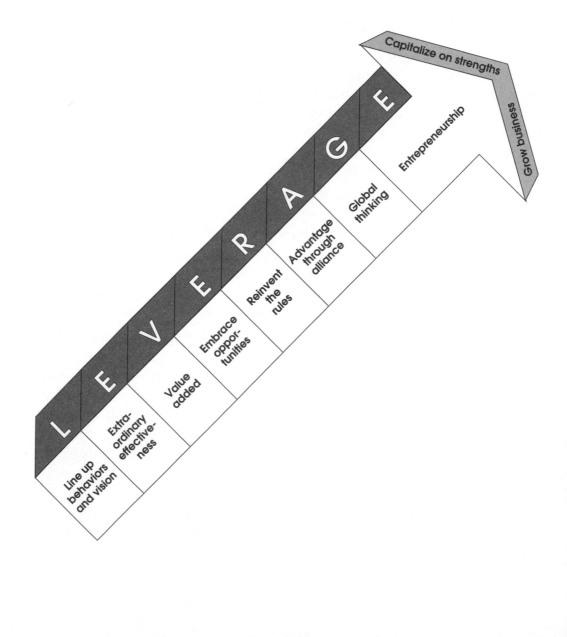

Line Up Behaviors and Vision

The congruency between everyday actions and your vision and values demonstrates what is truly important to the organization and how it will operate. Alignment demonstrates that the team's vision and values are genuine. Every action is an opportunity to make the vision tangible and to reinforce the direction.

Consistency between words and behaviors creates trust and bolsters credibility. When confusion or conflict arises between actions and vision, corporate energy is dissipated. Every action sends a signal. Individuals inside and outside the organization will observe how our stated values are reinforced.

- What behaviors, attitudes and outcomes are rewarded?

- What are the true (demonstrated) priorities? Cost? Quality? Customer service?

- How is time (and other resources) spent?

- What questions are asked and answered?

Program your team for success. Team leverage results from aligning group consciousness and actions. When our thoughts and actions are out of line, extra energy is required to respond to environmental pressures. Misalignment can result from imbalances of thoughts, behavioral patterns, or clarity of direction. Energy is wasted and fatigue sets in when confusion, uncertainty, and conflict occur.

Leverage requires a conscious decision to realign team patterns and to move corporate energy freely, steadily, and continuously in a specific direction. Successful teams create an environment to use and take advantage of collective energy and creativity. Our intentions gather and focus our energies in a set direction. If our intention is to create harmony, then our thoughts, words, and actions will create it. If our intention is spontaneity, then natural, uninhibited, instinctive actions will occur. Our intentions create our experience of reality. What we intend, we become!

Intentions set the environment for the law of commitment to apply. The moment we commit to a project or a way of being, we set in motion the forces that help us create it. Our decision focuses our attention like a laser beam and eliminates other choices and possibilities. Concentration enables us to notice and take advantage of opportunities as they occur.

Here are some ways to program your team for success:

- Create a positive group consciousness. Identify which parts of your environment you can control and look for the benefit or opportunity in every situation.

- Take time out to revitalize your spirit or attitude. Ask, "What keeps the dream alive?"

- Examine what you do. Step back to gain a new perspective. Change the process or the order in which you do things.

- Review your goals. Visualize desired results continually and focus on your intentions. Examine your goals to ensure they are in harmony with one another.

- Dedicate one-half hour per day for creative thinking. Use this time to explore and experiment with new ideas and to gain new insights.

- Get into the habit of expecting the best. Look for the good qualities in others and take time to recognize and appreciate individual contributions. Reward actions that strengthen shared aims and aspirations.

- Examine opportunities and make choices visible. Understand that mental attitude influences every experience we encounter and that it is transferred from one person to another.

- Enthusiasm is contagious—and one opportunity leads to another.

Extraordinary Effectiveness

Have you ever watched the graceful movements of a tennis player, figure skater, or gymnast and wondered how they make their sport look so easy? Have you noticed how precisely each motion leads to another? When an athlete is at the top of his game, every element comes together at the proper moment—intention, skill, thoughts, emotions, and actions. The performer is totally focused on the purpose of the moment. All irrelevant thoughts are set aside and his focus is locked on to what is essential in the moment. By creating this focus, the athlete remains open to emerging possibilities and can choose appropriate actions to ensure the desired results.

Make change work for you. The Chinese symbol for change consists of two parts, one meaning "danger" and the other "opportunity." Every change consists of positive and negative elements. To turn change into an advantage, choose to

- embrace change rather than resist it.
- learn to work with it rather than against it.
- develop the necessary skills to create opportunities.

Focus deliberately. Think long-term and create a climate that supports ongoing change. Encourage others to recognize opportunities by envisioning the future and developing a sense of what is uniquely possible. Tap into the natural energy of the moment—excitement, curiosity, passion and desire. Remember, the increased awareness of only a few people can greatly affect group consciousness!

Value Added

Value lies in the eye of the beholder—and it can change from one moment to the next. The value of any activity, experience, or idea is created by our perception of its benefit, our interpretation of the item's usefulness. Throughout the day we continually make choices by evaluating the value of our actions. Assigning value is a moment-by-moment choice.

As a customer, what factors come to mind when you think of receiving value for your money? You might think of such criteria as service, reliability, durability, or trouble-free maintenance. Value is situational. If you are trading in a reliable car for the latest model, you may perceive value in the most advanced technology available. On the other hand, if you have repeatedly repaired your old car, you may perceive more value in an extended warranty.

Educate your customer. Because value is a perception and perceptions constantly change, it is important to educate our customers on the benefits of our products or services. But first we must gain a clear understanding of our customer's needs and match those needs to our products in such a way that the benefits are easily identified and understood. The more immediate and concrete we can make the benefit, the easier it is to satisfy the customer.

In 1981, the U.S. airline industry was changing significantly. The market was going through deregulation and new no-frills carriers like People Express were adding options and lower prices to customers. The established airlines found themselves in a battle for passengers as customers pursued the lowest price.

To counteract eroding customer loyalty, American Airlines introduced its AAdvantage frequent flyer program—a program that allowed passengers to receive credits for each mile flown and to redeem these credits for free flights.

To create an even greater incentive to continue flying with them, American offered better rewards with more miles flown. In a sense, the program created loyalty by rewarding it.

This program revolutionized the industry in a number of ways. First, by restricting free travel to a limited number of seats on each plane, American had changed non-revenue-generating empty seats into an advantage. Second, the program was especially beneficial to American's most profitable customers— business travelers who could receive rewards for frequent usage.

The program was so successful in establishing customer loyalty that within three months all other major U.S. airlines had created their own frequent flyer programs. The programs created a win-win situation. They provided an advantage for the large airline over the regional carrier, and they offered customers free trips and provided a tax-free way for companies to compensate employees for business travel. Today the frequent flyer program has expanded to include car rental agencies, credit card companies, and hotels that provide more incentives for continuing to fly.

Transfer risk. Even after educating our customers, they may still be reluctant to buy. How can we overcome this resistance? First, we must understand that every transaction entails a risk—either real or imagined. We can add value to our products and services by transferring risk from our customers to ourselves in the form of a product guarantee. Standing behind our products builds trust and enhances our credibility. Once we have established a track record of reliability, the perception of risk is minimized in the minds of our customers.

Embrace Opportunities

One man's problem is another man's opportunity. Opportunity is a mindset, a way of thinking or seeing. Opportunities arise when we see situations from a multidimensional perspective. When we look at issues from different points of view, on many sides and many levels, we discover that opportunities are everywhere. Every business activity, every relationship and every context contain the seeds of opportunity.

Develop your opportunity thinking by expanding your exposure to other industries, businesses, and strategies. Notice what works and what doesn't. Observe how focus or intention impacts results. Identify the most viable and adaptable concepts and evaluate which ones have the greatest potential for transfer to your business.

Open your mind and explore different perspectives by studying the ideas and insights of successful people. You don't have to reinvent the wheel. Learn from others' experiences. Notice similarities and differences to your situation. Extrapolate ideas that have the most potential for you and test them in your environment.

Generate new ideas by combining old elements in new ways to create new ideas and applications. Insights are created by curiosity, concentration, and focus. Decide to look for insights, relationship linkages, and commonalities. Dare to be unconventional—don't be afraid to look foolish. Take opposite points of view and let go of your expectations. Stay grounded in the present moment and notice the ideas, thoughts, and insights that surface.

Take time to nurture ideas. Allow an idea to grow, percolate, and expand. Activate your conscious and subconscious mind by shifting your focus to something different—something you enjoy, such as a hobby, sport, or leisure activity. Often new ideas and insights appear when we are not consciously focused on solving a problem.

Reinvent the rules

Rules define how we play the game. They are the boundaries and limits that we create to bring order to our environment. Rules set the parameters of how we perceive, think, and feel about a situation and thus affect how we respond. Remember, you make the rules you play by!

Reinventing the rules requires a willingness to move out of our comfort zones—a willingness to look at and free up your locked-in thinking that has been created by your past experiences, beliefs, assumptions and focus. When we apply intuition and logic, we create new vantage points; when we challenge existing assumptions, we establish new perspectives. We can then apply these new perspectives to develop new strategies and tactics for creating the results we desire.

By changing the way we see our business, we can establish a new set of rules and create a new game. Start with an attitude of curiosity and excitement. Look at your present situation and ask yourself, "How does it work? What's working well? How do I know it works well?"

Then take a step back and evaluate your answers with fresh eyes. Look at the big picture and ask yourself, "What's unique or different? What are our strengths?" Create a childlike innocence by exploring the situation without preconceived ideas. Draw a visual map of each of the key elements—how they fit together and how they work together or complement each other. Look at the picture and ask, "What strengths are we not using? What could we do differently?"

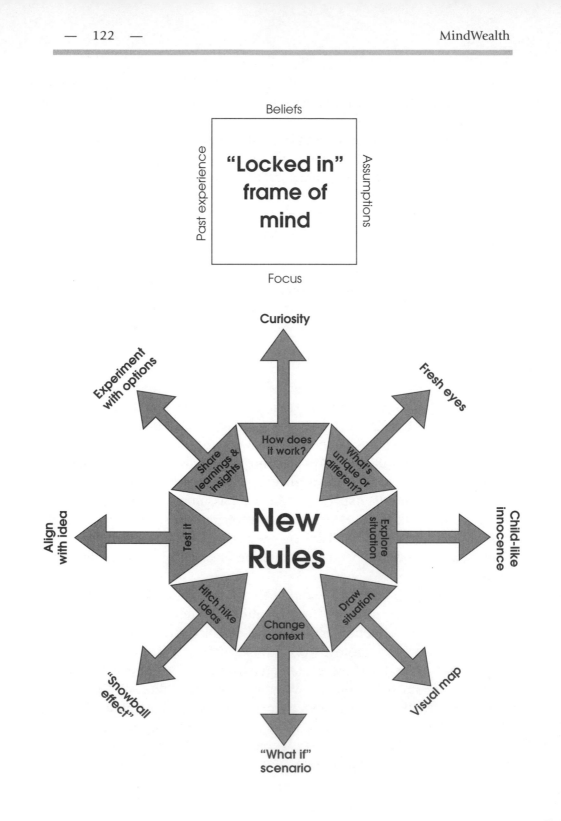

Next, develop "what if" scenarios by brainstorming other ways to approach a solution. Create a snowball effect by hitchhiking on each other's ideas.

Align with an idea and test it. Look at the implications and effects of implementing your idea—the skills needed, processes required, and resources available. Explore options by challenging your assumptions. Determine and clarify which rules are important and which are not. Record and share your insights and perceptions.

Play your own game. By creating new rules, you open up a whole new range of possibilities—new ways to use technology or create new products, new ways to leverage your customer base and distribution channels. These new ways define a new game built on your strengths and uniqueness.

As you experiment with various options, remember that rules are guidelines not absolutes. An effective rule today may not work tomorrow. Be willing to continually redefine the rules. There are no right or wrong ways to do business—only what is effective in the moment. When you face obstacles, redefine them as opportunities to see your business in a new way and to challenge old beliefs and assumptions.

Advantage through Alliance

We can create leverage in today's competitive global markets by establishing partnerships with other groups and organizations. Alliances are mutually beneficial relationships that open up possibilities that would not have existed for either partner acting alone. Through alliances, an organization may gain new technological expertise, faster access to new markets, or better utilization of resources.

Knowledge links are partnerships or alliances developed for the purpose of creating synergistic learning environments where lessons and insights are shared in order to improve work practices to match industry bests and incorporate into daily operations. The process can be one of benchmarking issues, functions, or processes, or one of creating new competencies by sharing experience, insights, and information.

Alliances can occur inside or outside an organization and at many levels. The key ingredient is a mutual need or desire to enter into an agreement that creates a synergy or multiplied value through a connection of products, services, technology, information, or resources.

As long as I have something you need and you have something I need, an opportunity exists for a mutually beneficial alliance. The key to opening new avenues of cooperation is a willingness to acknowledge each other's strengths and weaknesses and the ability to utilize each other's tangible and intangible assets.

Intangible assets are such things as relationships with vendors, suppliers, or customers which have been cultivated for years but which are often overlooked. One of the most important principles of leverage is that every relationship has a tangible value. Every person and every organization has a sphere of influence. Every cooperative relationship opens the door to new spheres of influence.

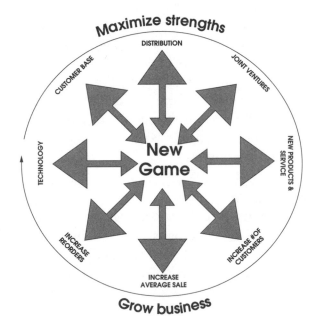

Go beyond the rules of tradition. Look at your relationships from a different point of view. Reverse relationships in your mind. Instead of thinking about what a supplier provides you, look at what you could provide the supplier. Ask, "How can I use this relationship more fully? What are potential benefits dependent upon?"

Continually challenge your underlying assumptions by asking "Why?" Suspend judgment of new ideas by asking "What is useful in this idea? What can I learn from this?" Identify the most viable and adaptable concepts and evaluate them for potential results. Concentrate your focus on the key ideas and determine their applicability to your business.

Build a bridge of understanding by sharing your experience, thoughts, feelings, and perceptions. Develop trust and rapport by looking for common ground. Be willing to assume responsibility for co-creation of the moment. Focus your intention on creating support and linkage by asking open-ended, probing questions. Keep your focus on actions and behaviors rather than personalities.

Build a bridge between thoughts and actions by creating the habit of finishing what you start. If environmental conditions create a change of direction, take action to link the old and the new and to preserve work already done.

Global Thinking

Leverage is created when organizations are viewed as open systems that dynamically interact, respond, and create their environments. View organizations holistically—as units that comprise a complex web of multi-level relationships. Each element is interdependent and each component affects the other.

When we view everything as interconnected, it is easier to recognize how change in one part influences other parts. Focusing exclusively on a single element leads to suboptimal results or new problems. Change must be approached from a bigger or broader perspective. We cannot change subsystems in isolation. Instead, we must pay attention to how individual elements interact with the system and the environment. This shift in perspective is the same process we go through as individuals when we move from reaction to co-creation. When we acknowledge that everything is interconnected, we begin to understand that we create the problems we experience—and we hold the solution to every problem as well.

A global mind-set recognizes that every organization is self-organizing. Order and structure are not imposed by the environment but are developed through the organization's internal focus and desires. Self-organizing systems have the power to renew and transform themselves. They have the ability to regenerate themselves within their original structure, or to transform themselves by expanding beyond their present boundaries to evolve to a higher level.

Self-organizing systems constantly create homeostasis, or balance between adaptation and creation. Interaction with the environment constantly tests the stability of the system. Because all levels in the system are interdependent, internal and external forces will be felt throughout the system.

Conversely, every action to modify and create the desired environmental conditions will ripple through all levels of the organization.

Each interface is a process of mutual influence. All situations are co-created. The patterns we see around us are created from the patterns within our minds. For example, when we're unclear about our goals or values, our inter-actions and discussions become confused. By consciously choosing to alter our behaviors, perceptions, or values, we can shape our environment and change our experience of reality. When we become aware of our perceptions and acknowledge our feelings, the level of rapport and trust increases as we shift control from our heads to our hearts.

Our mind-set creates opportunities. When we think globally by looking at a situation from a higher vantage point and exploring the interconnections between activities, processes, and behaviors, new opportunities become obvious. The key is to let go of our preconceived ideas about how things should be, and to simply observe what is happening around us. These obser-vations allow us to choose new directions.

Anticipation is the process of interpreting recurring patterns and taking advantage of them. During the 1980s, I watched Wayne Gretzky play hockey for the Edmonton Oilers. One day a reporter asked Gretzky how he was able to "get free so often." Gretzky replied, "I don't go where the puck is, I go to where the puck will be." By looking at the big picture and understanding the how the flow of the game interconnected with positioning and angles on the ice, Gretzky was able to anticipate other players' moves and create opportuni-ties to score. By observing trends in our businesses, our communities, and in society, we can see changes, notice trends, and anticipate opportunities for ourselves. Begin to broaden your information intake by watching documen-taries, listening to call-in programs, and reading a variety of magazine articles. Use everyday activities to gain more insights. Observe people on the subway; notice fashions in department stores; or walk through a bookstore and note prominently displayed titles and popular topics.

Entrepreneurship

In his book *The Global Paradox,* John Naisbitt talks about changes in the global economy and the shifts necessary for survival. He predicts that by the turn of the century "only small and medium-size companies or big companies that have restyled themselves as networks of entrepreneurs will be viable." His prediction appears accurate when we look at recent economic trends in job creation and economic growth. While corporate America continues to downsize, restructure and re-engineer, entrepreneurs are driving and stimulating the economy.

Will your organization be able to adapt and survive in this new economy? What will you need to do to compete? How will you need to change? To ensure your corporate survival, you will need to understand and develop an entrepreneurial spirit.

Entrepreneurship is a process of creating something of value—finding a need and filling it or anticipating a need and filling it. It's the pursuit of opportunities that requires vision, commitment and a willingness to take risks.

Entrepreneurs are independent and self-reliant, and they share the following characteristics:

- Internal motivation and drive. They have a passion or excitement to create something of value.

- Confidence. They believe they can handle any situation.

- Focus on improvement. They look for ways to do things better. They are not satisfied with the status quo.

- Convert failures into learning experiences. They believe the game is never over. There is always time to prepare, adjust and move forward.

- Identify opportunities by using intuition based on an accumulation of experiences.

- Use every situation to explore new possibilities and ideas.

- Continue to create and explore new ideas.

Invest in the future now. To create entrepreneurial activities decide to

- Develop a do-it-now mentality. Entrepreneurs build decisiveness into their work by making decisions and being committed. They learn how to adapt their approaches while maintaining the same direction.

- Use other people's experience by developing partnerships that provide new strengths or advantages. Realize that you don't need to be an expert at everything!

- Cultivate an idea-friendly environment where individuals are encouraged to be creative.

- Think backwards. Imagine the result first and then create the product.

- Create a culture of innovation and be willing to take risks to succeed. One breakthrough can spawn generations of other ideas and businesses.

- Talk to successful entrepreneurs about their experiences to find out their beliefs, how they perceive challenges, and what works and what doesn't.

It takes less energy to keep on climbing
than it does to hang onto a ledge.

—John R. Noe

Part III

Achieve Organization Synergy

No act of kindness, no matter how small,
is ever wasted.

—Aesop

Listening is a form of accepting.

—Stella Terrill Mann

Chapter 13

Build Community

It was not unusual for an individual of my father's generation to live in the same house and work for the same company for his entire career. Today it's more likely that a person will have three or four careers and will work for a number of companies—perhaps moving across country in the process.

Living in an urban center and working for a large corporation create a sense of isolation—a separation from meaningful experiences and interactions. Often, the larger the organization and the more change that occurs, the greater the feeling of alienation.

The acceleration of technology in the information age and the rapidly expanding global marketplace have created a fundamental transformation in the way we do business. For many years, organizations maintained an illusion of innovation by jumping on the bandwagon of the latest quick fix, whether it was a technological breakthrough or change initiatives like re-engineering or total quality management.

However, as the survivors of mergers and downsizings struggled to cope with all the changes, it became obvious that the new way to do business had not created the results expected. Often the attempt to become lean and mean did not significantly improve the organization's speed or flexibility. Instead, it resulted in disillusionment, uncertainty, and inhibited risk-taking.

It's time we created a new community that establishes integration and togetherness—a sense of moving in the same direction, feeling supported and connected. This feeling of community doesn't occur instantly but rather grows from a continuously evolving spirit of oneness. The following diagram depicts the key components of this evolution:

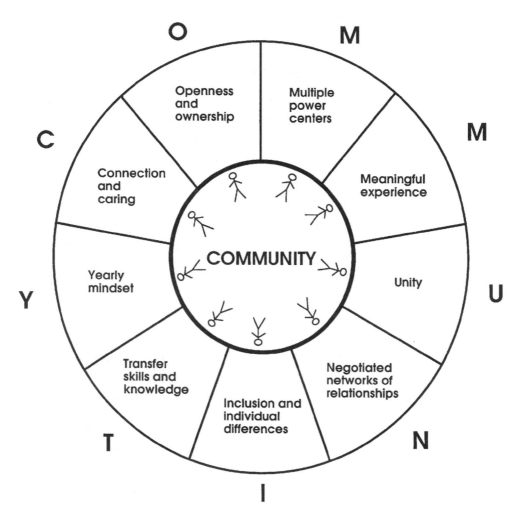

Connection and Caring

The key foundation to building a community is the creation of a caring, connected environment. This environment is based on trust and acceptance of individual differences. Trust is developed over time through consistent actions. Handle it with care: once trust has been violated or broken, it is not easily recreated. Broken trust requires specific, deliberate actions to re-establish and reconnect rapport.

For example, the president of a company that had just gone through a downsizing asked me to come in to help with team and community building. Initially, he thought that a viable community could be established through a few team-building exercises. But once we started to talk about the purpose of the one-day sessions, he began to understand that the real issue was how to re-establish trust and build cooperative connections between downsized divisions and departments. Because trust had been destroyed through the downsizing process, community building would take time.

Because the old, familiar networks and relationships had been undermined, we designed our sessions with the purpose of reconnecting the survivors of the downsizing. Processes were focused around the following key principles:

1. Start where the group is. Let the feelings and concerns of the group direct the discussion. Often, companies make the mistake of trying to begin where the managers and leaders think the group "ought" to be. Starting with preconceived ideas of the emotional and interpersonal dynamics of a group can further alienate team members and reinforce mistrust of the leaders.

2. Rebuild rapport by listening without judgment to the concerns, issues, and feelings expressed by group members. If the leaders respond defensively to expressions of feeling let down or betrayed, the foundation for trust-building will be further undermined.

3. Acknowledge individual concerns and discuss new beginnings by exploring how the downsizing will affect the group's roles, tasks, and work levels.

4. Explore new ways of working together and discuss insights, necessary adjustments, and new directions.

These steps are only the first of many along the pathway to community. Although they will open a dialogue and start the reconnection process, they are not a panacea. Individuals will continue to struggle to make sense of the new direction and will need time to understand their new roles. Part of the cost of change—especially dramatic or catastrophic change—is the need for time and patience to allow the assimilation process to run its course. Organizations that seek to rush through the change process often fall into the trap of imposing standards. As we discussed earlier, externally imposed change is less likely to succeed than changes that are internally motivated.

Before a community spirit can be developed, a caring environment must be created. It simply takes time—often several seasons—to establish an environment where individuals feel supported and appreciated and where experimenting with new ways of being is encouraged.

This environment is often advanced more quickly through the little things done in day-to-day operations than through the company's declared values. I remember the first time I witnessed the effect that the little things can have on creating a community spirit—a spirit of caring and togetherness. I was a manager in a large organization and we were opening a new multimillion-dollar facility. We were working hard to meet the deadline of the official opening date. There was frantic activity and everyone was putting in extra effort and time so that we would be ready for the company officials who were coming in from across the country.

Hours before the opening, I stopped to take a rest and to look at the last-minute details that needed to be completed. I suddenly realized that only senior managers were invited to the opening receptions—the support staff who had worked so hard were not included.

The receptions were set and could not be changed, but there was a need to recognize the efforts of the supporting cast. I sent my assistant to buy roses and a vase for every employee as a small appreciation of a job well done. The cost was insignificant in the scope of the total budget, but the effect was amazing. For weeks afterward, my colleagues continued to comment about the roses and what it had meant to receive them. They felt appreciated and part of the team. Generally, people want to feel that their contributions are valued and their efforts are appreciated. This appreciation doesn't have to be big. It can be a smile, a rose, a word of acknowledgment of a job well done, or a special recognition.

Openness and Ownership

Community-building and relationship-building are one and the same. After all, a community is nothing more than a group of individuals united in relationships based on commonality. A community can only be developed if there is open and authentic communication. A caring atmosphere is created when people feel safe to be themselves, to communicate differing points of view, and to express feelings that will be listened to and accepted.

Openness requires a willingness to be vulnerable; to communicate honestly with each other by letting go of the facade or masks of position, knowledge or expertise; and to be present and authentic in the moment. It requires a commitment to one another and a willingness to stick together through all the ups and downs of life. It includes appreciating and celebrating differences among individuals.

When we choose to understand and deal with differing expectations and perceptions, and to look at how to accept and appreciate individual differences, we open ourselves to see how these differences weave a pattern that gives strength to the whole.

To be authentic means to own and accept our personal power—the power within—and how it creates our experiences. It means acknowledging our anxiety, fears, and concerns, and understanding that each moment is created by the choices we make. When a safe place is created for expressing these emotions, our resistance and defenses come down and healing of old wounds can occur. By being open to the experience of every moment and experimenting with new behaviors, we can discover new rules and new states of consciousness.

Multiple Power Centers

A safe environment for open and authentic interaction is established through equality of inclusion and participation. When each member of a group feels important and respected, leadership can shift as situations and tasks change. When power is shared and functional leadership is allowed to flow to the individual who is best qualified in each situation, the performance of the team is optimized, fresh ideas begin to flow, and the goals of the group become achievable. When multiple power centers of leadership exist, control becomes a function of expertise and the requirements of the work flow process. Flexibility is enhanced as individuals move in and out of positions of leadership. Everyone participates in the creative process and decision making occurs through informed consensus.

This flow requires a shift in the paradigm of leadership. In *The Different Drum,* Scott Peck aptly observes that "communities have sometimes been referred to as leaderless groups. It is more accurate, however, to say that a community is a group of all leaders."

Distributed leadership creates a sequence of roles and shared behaviors, which are rotated and used as necessary. At any one time multiple leaders may be functioning, with each leader assuming a complementary role in the overall group dynamic.

When new groups are assembled or project ideas are being developed, there is often a higher need for formal leadership or direction than once the project has taken form. As the group the group takes shape and initiates a dialogue, ownership is created and roles begin to emerge at the proper time. Usually, individual members will initiate directions in the areas of their expertise. The strong right-brain thinkers will visualize the big picture and begin to generate ideas. Someone with strong organizing skills will sort the information and outline a plan. The strong critical thinkers will suggest revisions and refinements, while others will turn the idea on its head and suggest new approaches or new possibilities.

For this type of leadership to be effective, the rules for working together, as well as the roles and processes, must be flexible. Teams must be organized to facilitate the work flow process rather than by specific functional tasks. For example, a project team created to develop a new product would also be involved in developing marketing strategies, because they are the ones who fully understand the product's capabilities.

Meaningful Experience

Leadership is rarely easy. It requires a willingness to step out and to trust the moment, with the understanding that everything happens for a reason. Effective leadership is based on the knowledge that we each create the life we want—deliberately, if we choose to accept the responsibility, or by default if we shirk our responsibility.

For shared leadership to be successful, each individual must believe that he or she can contribute and that their contributions will be rewarding. This means we must overcome a series of double binds between belief and action. We have a tradition of competition, but to succeed we must cooperate. We feel pressure to get the job done efficiently, but we also believe that all points of view must be heard, and that the best ideas often come late in the process. Quick decisions are often necessary, yet we value participatory decision-making. Each of these issues creates a potential barrier to distributing leadership, ownership, and responsibility.

Distributed leadership assumes that each member has certain leadership qualities that will be needed periodically by the group. The flow of leadership depends on the discovery and coordination of a team's untapped resources, which will only occur in an environment where individual differences are respected, cultivated, and constructively employed. Distributed leadership presents a unique challenge, because it increases the potential for conflict. Every group, regardless of size or skill, must confront and resolve conflict in order to develop as a community.

A number of years ago, I was part of a consulting project to design a community-building activity based on valuing differences within a group.

Each project team member had experience in group dynamics, team-building, facilitation, and training, so there was no shortage of ideas about how to design and create the session. After a lot of discussion, we decided to split into pairs to design specific components and activities before getting back together as a group to finalize the design.

My partner and I were responsible for designing the final activity of the session, which would also function as a bridge to another community building retreat. As she and I began to design our process, we realized that we could not design an effective program if our own group didn't value differences.

When the full group reconvened to finalize the design, my partner and I raised the issue of non-congruency between the project team's mission and its practice. As you can imagine, our comments ignited a spirited discussion about what it meant to value differences.

Throughout the discussion, we asked ourselves the following questions: How are we valuing differences right now? What's important in this process? What can we learn from this? As we continued to explore the topic, we gained valuable insights that significantly changed the structure, content, and design of the session. Months later, the client continued to refer to that particular session as the turning point for his division.

It was also a turning point for us as consultants. It raised our level of awareness, strengthened our commitment to each other, and helped us grow as a community. In the process, we reinforced our understanding of several key principles of effective community development:

- Make an emotional investment in yourself and others. Commit yourself to creating a workplace that meets everyone's needs.

- Take ownership of creation. It's everyone's task to create a vision and translate it into action.

- Act from your heart to create the kind of culture you desire.

- Foster an environment where every individual has the right to act and speak and discover their own voice.

- Accept internal accountability for outcomes. Ask yourself, "How are my actions creating this situation?"

- Move from dependency to self-creation through a willingness to give up your need for safety.

- Stretch your boundaries and grow by trusting others. Remember, change starts the moment we decide to make the change.

Unity

Have you ever noticed how people rally together during a disaster such as an earthquake, flood, or tornado? Strangers help strangers and neighbors help neighbors—and everyone bonds in the moment of a common experience. The shift to what is important is effortless, because at that moment survival is more critical than any differences. People act instinctively to assess the moment and make decisions. All preconceived ideas and conditioning are secondary. Support is given and received. Emphasis shifts to finding solutions for problems by evaluating ideas against a standard of importance. In other words, all the team-building activities and cooperative techniques that we struggle to implement in our workday world, we naturally do in times of crisis.

If pulling together is such a natural process in times of dire need, we ought to be able to recreate a similar togetherness under more stable conditions. Yet political and cultural actions often block unity from occurring. How can togetherness occur? Use the suggestions below to help create a unified community.

Identify what is important by clarifying the most meaningful and valuable part of being a group or organization. Establish a focus or rallying point by creating a reason for being. Visualize the level of support and interaction you desire.

Let community evolve. A community is a tapestry of personalities, cultures, ideas and emotions. It is created through a web of relationships. Each relationship requires a blending of intimacy and individuality, of sharing experiences, emotions, and personalities.

Create trust by developing a mutual understanding and common concern for each other as individuals. When we de-emphasize the power issues inherent in our organizations and instead focus our attention on each other's strengths and experience, we create a context for closeness. Plan specific times and activities to renew community spirit and to share feelings without judgment or expectations.

Create support structures and invite growth experiences. Community involves both separation and togetherness. Even when we are apart, we are together on another level through understanding and acceptance. By sharing our dreams, exploring painful moments, and noticing ways in which we unconsciously protect ourselves, we transcend to a new level of communication, encouragement and support.

Use rituals to create special moments of sharing. Use a common greeting, a poem, or a prayer to honor and celebrate the journey and sustain the emotional desire to move forward. Develop a celebration of wholeness where you collectively honor each other. For example, start each meeting with a ritual of giftgiving by giving the gift of affirmation and gratitude. Explain what you appreciate about the person next to you, or have each person explain what they are grateful for as a member of the group.

Building unity occurs moment by moment as we weave individual needs and desires together into a common direction. Establish an environment where individuals are invited to stretch and grow. Encourage expression and sharing. Allow each person to choose his or her own level of participation—the level of sharing, the choice of feedback, and the decision to take risks. The key is to establish boundaries that allow people to move out of their comfort zones and explore new behaviors.

Adapt unifying activities to the level of openness and trust in the group, and tailor processes to fit the issues to be addressed. Below are some helpful processes to center each person into the present moment:

Check-in

Start with a check-in procedure. Ask each person to describe how they feel or what they need at this moment. This process can be structured as a one-word check-in, a one-sentence check-in, or a detailed description.

Create a physical continuum by using a check-in process that requires an answer to a specific question and a physical demonstration of the answer. For example, I may ask you to rate your level of participation in yesterday's session on a continuum from zero to one hundred percent, with zero signifying total displeasure and one hundred representing total satisfaction. Once you have assigned a numerical value to your level, you move physically to stand in the area of the room that represents your level on the continuum.

The benefit of this activity is that it creates a visual representation of the group, and it can be interactive. Once everyone is in position, ask them to discuss with the people next to them why they placed themselves at that level. Then facilitate a group discussion about the implications of the group's configuration. This technique can be used to raise issues for further discussion.

Group Mapping

Assemble a physical group map. Although this process is similar to creating a physical continuum, it does not answer a specific question. Instead, its purpose is to create a visual representation of a group's characteristics. These characteristics can be anything that affects how the group is working together.

For example, I might ask people to move to different parts of the room in relation to their functional areas such as sales, marketing, and information systems. Then I ask them to move to a new configuration based on organizational levels such as management, support staff, and sales. Then I ask everyone to move again into groups representing product lines. Between each move, I ask people to observe the group and identify issues, concerns, and blockages that impact the way the group works.

Statements of Intention

Ask each group member to state an intention for the activity or session. This technique helps each person identify her needs and take a conscious step to create what she wants to experience. For example, one person might say, "I intend to enjoy the process," or "I intend to open myself to my creativity." Each statement energizes and directs their thoughts into action.

Statements of Gratitude

In this process, each group member explains what he appreciates and is grateful for in his life. This activity can be open-ended to include any aspect of life, or it can be focused on group activities. For example, one might say, "I'm grateful for my family," or if the focus is on group dynamics, he might say, "I'm grateful for the opportunity to receive feedback."

Group Centering

Ground the group's energy by making a conscious connection between the group and surrounding physical space. Ask each member to visualize a large group grounding cord—a hollow, flowing cord that attaches to the center of the Earth. Instruct the group to release emotions of frustration down the cord and visualize them flowing away. Invite the group members to think of the feelings that they want to experience and visualize the situation that way.

This exercise is also useful for refocusing the group after conflict or confusion has occurred.

Negotiated Network of Relationships

A community is a web of relationships—an open, changing system that is affected by internal and external factors. Community evolves through trust and intimacy and is maintained through the enhancement of each member's personal sense of worth.

Each relationship provides us with a unique way of looking at and experiencing life. Each interaction creates a connection of acceptance and recognition of who we are. Each experience asks us to examine what we believe and what we stand for. Our relationships are a reflection of ourselves. When we are in conflict with another person, we are really in conflict with ourselves. When we change our awareness, our relationships with the outside world change.

We bring a set of conscious and subconscious values and expectations to every experience, which create a pattern of interaction. This pattern sets the boundaries that define who participates in our relationships and how. The law of complementarity flows constantly through every interaction. All situations are co-created. We are both creators of and created by our current context. That is, the behavior of one person calls forth and makes possible the behavior of another person. For example, a supervisor's lack of direction results in a subordinate's lack of making direct requests.

Each interaction is a reflection of our needs. What we do and how we do it teach others how to treat us. If I want respect, I must respect you. If I want you to listen to my ideas, I must listen to yours.

Each relationship is a negotiation of boundaries between ourselves and others. Each boundary is a set of values and expectations, both conscious and subconscious, that we attempt to fulfill in the interaction. These boundaries set the rules of the interaction, but our level of effectiveness is determined by our ability to move between clear and blurry boundaries. Each moment is constantly asking us to clarify what is important and why. When we bring our awareness to the relationship and open our hearts to the experience, we can change the world around us.

One of the most difficult aspects of changing a relationship is setting new boundaries. I must first be clear about what I want to be different. Then I must be willing to communicate my needs effectively and work through the issues that will arise once the boundary is set.

I've learned over the years that the more clearly and specifically I communicate what I want, the more likely it is that the new boundary will be mutually acceptable. But if I don't communicate clearly, the other person's response will reflect my confusion and will challenge me to re-examine my belief. Sometimes the most difficult part of setting a boundary is staying firm about what I want and believing I deserve to have the life I envision.

Every relationship is a negotiation, a give and take that allows for all parties to meet their important needs. But effective relationships occur only when we do these things:

- Clearly and calmly communicate our needs.

- Respect the other person and their position.

- Intend to create mutual benefits.

- Open to alternative actions.

- Let go of hurts and offenses.

Inclusion and Individual Differences

Individual differences within a group are the strengths of a community. Blending together differences gives a community its uniqueness. Community-building requires a balance between individual and group needs. It is a process of accepting, acknowledging, and utilizing individual differences, and channeling these differences to help each individual discover his or her own unique gifts.

In order to strengthen its manufacturing facilities and to develop new products G.E. Plastics purchased Borg-Warner Chemicals in 1988. Both companies had excellent workforces but, the cultures were significantly different. There was a need to create trust and loyalty and to develop a way that the two work forces could become a single team.

Joel Hutt, manager of marketing communications, was part of a team in charge of organizing G.E.'s corporate meetings. He wanted a team-building experience that would create a lasting impression while serving a larger purpose. He wondered if it was possible to take 400 to 500 people and create an activity that would be constructive and helpful to other people. This led to a powerful, innovative team-building activity called "Share to Gain."

The purpose of the activity was to provide lasting benefits to the community through teamwork by renovating nonprofit facilities such as YMCA's and homeless shelters. To start the renovations the division was divided into thirty preselected teams consisting of a mixture of Borg-Warner and G.E. employees. The groups created team names and selected project leaders. Each team was assigned a specific task and given a detailed description and list of materials.

Over the next twelve hours, the project teams replaced stained carpet, scraped and painted walls and ceilings, laid tile, and landscaped grounds. At first teams were competing against each other, but by the end teams who had finished their work helped others. The result was a win-win for both the community and the company—employees worked together toward a shared goal, and dilapidated facilities that served the entire community were renovated.

To start a community-building process, ask the following questions:

- What talents and skills do I bring to the group?
- What are our strengths and uniqueness as a group?
- What are the characteristics and qualities of the kind of community I desire?
- What stands in our way of establishing community?
- What do we as individuals need to give up in order to form a community?

Discussing these questions allows the group to explore and confront the following issues of balance.

Autonomy versus interdependence: Each individual must have the freedom to do her own thing, to take risks and to grow and learn, yet there must be value placed on mutual support and peer relationships.

In*dividual versus group contribution:* Individuals must be able to contribute in a meaningful, significant way that recognizes and develops their talents while contributing to the betterment of the whole group.

Influence versus emotional association: Group members must be able to influence the decision-making process and to share in each other's experience and wisdom. Each member must be free to contribute ideas, raise concerns, and provide suggestions as part of the decision-making process.

A genuine community is not easily achieved or maintained. In order to create a strong community, there must be a willingness to set aside or transcend individual interests, when appropriate, for the interests of the group. At the same time, each contribution must be treated equally and every individual's talents must be celebrated, which can only occur when ideas are shared, valued, and respected.

To create a community bond, our interactions must move from "what I think" to "how I feel." Bonding requires openness and vulnerability, and true connection can only occur when the dialogue shifts from the head to the heart. When someone talks about his feelings, I can listen with my heart because I too have had pain, frustration, and unfulfilled dreams. This opening to a different level of understanding and compassion can create a bridge from one heart to another.

In my master's degree program, we were taught that "self as an instrument" was more important than any tool or technique of intervention. And although I have used this principle for many years, only recently have I truly understood its power. When I reveal my *self,* I move from the head to the heart. I shift the discussion and set the environment for a different level of rapport. By sharing my experiences, I can help others to understand theirs.

You can increase rapport through a progressive level of sharing.

Step 1. Self-observation. By sharing in the moment, you acknowledge the situation as it is and honor the experience. This allows you to own your own perceptions and actions and to put your emotions into words. For example, you might say, "I'm disappointed in the way this project is progressing," or "I'm nervous about the speech tomorrow."

Step 2. Observation of others. By sharing what you see and hear you provide information to others that allows them to see the situation from a different perspective. For example, you might say, "Just before you started to answer my question, I saw you hesitate and look away."

Step 3. Comment on content or process. By sharing your ideas and thoughts, you can help others interpret and evaluate events differently. In turn, you can gain insight into new ways of thinking and acting.

Each of these levels of discussion creates opportunities for mutually increased awareness, which in turn creates opportunities to make new choices and decisions. When rapport is built through open and honest discussion, individual differences can be blended together to create a common bond—a "cooperative" advantage that cannot be matched by other teams or organizations.

However, as we open ourselves to a deeper understanding and appreciation of one another, we may also open the door to conflict when misunderstandings occur. We must commit ourselves to resolve such conflicts as they happen and to accept conflict as part of the group process.

Ask your group to agree in advance to a set of ground rules. You might find the following rules useful:

- Deal with differences as they occur. Handle small disagreements of concept, ideas, perceptions, and divergent goals before they escalate into larger conflicts.

- Produce an intention to create a win-win discussion. Respect each other's needs and perceptions.

- Focus the discussion on specific areas of concern that can be acted upon. Keep the discussion centered on issues that the individual or group can influence or control.

- Take responsibility for your perceptions and ideas. Use "I" statements and remember that each situation is co-created.

- Look for similarities or common ground. Focus on understanding the other person's position.

- Use the process of "think and listen" to develop understanding. One person listens and thinks about what is said without interrupting to make comments or ask questions.

Transfer Skills and Knowledge

Peak performing organizations build on and take advantage of expertise and knowledge gained over time. Innovation and continuous improvement occur when lessons of the past are blended with opportunities in the present.

The past can create a road map and point the way to the future. But for this to occur, there must be a cultural mind-set that values the lessons of the past and looks for ways to use them. By looking back on what worked, what didn't work and why, the past sets a context for new strategies and new ideas.

When the future is supported by the past, a win-win situation is created. The person passing on the knowledge feels worthwhile and able to contribute, and the receiver gains insight that could not be developed without experience.

As organizations struggle to deal with competition in a global economy, this type of sharing becomes critical. In an environment of technological changes and shortened product lifespans, the company that can adapt quickly will have the advantage.

In order to remain competitive in the changing airline industry, American Airlines designed a suggestion program called IdeAA's in Action to capture the creativity and knowledge of its workers. Its focus was to find new ways to control expenses and generate new revenues by implementing actions that created savings. This program has become an integral part of the company's operation and has provided substantial savings yearly. In 1996, this initiative saved the company over $43 million.

Each year, savings occur over a wide range of operations—cost reduction in maintenance through the use of different parts and tools; savings of fuel by lobbying for and obtaining permission to fly directly over a closed restricted air force base, and savings on items included or changed in thousands of meals delivered daily.

The program is supported by IdeAAdvocates, individual volunteers who have agreed to be front-line representatives of IdeAA's in Action in their home areas. A person in this position is not eligible to submit suggestions but receives bonuses on accepted ideas. The position is for one year and is perceived as a opportunity for growth and as a step toward a management position. Each person is trained in the process and focuses on how to turn complaints into proposals. This provides the individual the opportunity to learn more about how the company operates as well as to deal with multiple functions and levels of the company.

IdeAA's in Action has been catalyst for pulling the company together. In 1991, IdeAA's in Flight, a $50 million fund drive, was created. The goal was to buy American's fiftieth Boeing 757 with the money saved. The plane became the symbol for working together and the power of ideas. By year's end, a total of $58 million in cost-saving ideas had been implemented.

The company had a "Name the Plane" contest and selected the name, "Pride of American" to be painted on the nose of the plane. The official launch became a three-day celebration, and whenever it flies, the plane reminds employees of the potential their ideas can have on the organization.

Yearly Mind-Set

Building community is an ongoing, evolving process that occurs year round. Every decision, every involvement, and every interaction make a statement about the commitment of the group to create a strong community. It's important to establish opportunities to build community into day-to-day operations. Here are some suggestions of ways to incorporate building community into your daily activities:

- Allocate time in meeting agendas to share lessons learned and build for the future.

- Use strategic planning sessions as an opportunity for teams or individuals to get to know and understand each other.

- Keep track of milestone achievements and set aside specific times to celebrate them as a whole community.

- Acknowledge and reward outstanding behavior that contributes to success.

- Assign group members to develop community-building activities and to provide input on group rewards.
- Use the surrounding environment to display the achievements of working together.

Each of our acts makes a statement
as to our purpose.

—Leo Buscaglia

You manage within a paradigm.
You lead between paradigms.

—Joel Barker

I find the great thing in this world
is not so much where we stand,
as in what direction we are moving.

—Oliver Wendell Holmes

Chapter 14

Transformative Power

Touch tomorrow - "teach"
Revitalize and recreate a new reality
Articulate a new direction
New leadership for a new world
Strengthen through self renewal
Future building through today's actions
Orchestrate optimum effectiveness
Revolutionary cultural change
Maintain momentum

Don Casson

An electrical transformer translates one type of energy into another. It changes and converts a source of energy into a workable voltage. At the large systems level of a company, transformative power acts as a converter or catalyst to unleash the power within the organization. Transformative power develops leadership and ownership at all levels.

Touch Tomorrow: Teach

We can touch the future by transferring the knowledge and insights gained through our experiences. When we teach and share our ideas and skills, we create a new direction. We can help others transform themselves into something different by exploring, expanding, and changing their thoughts, actions, and behaviors.

What we teach also teaches us. In order to guide another, we must clearly understand what is important and why. In order to communicate effectively to others, we must tap into and touch our own dreams. Teaching allows us to keep our dreams alive—by passing our dreams to another, who in turn can pass it on to someone else. By teaching, we can shape, mold, and create the future.

Every situation, interaction, or discussion can be used to teach by example. When we live our dreams regardless of the stresses and situations we face, we show others, through our behavior, that we live our values.

On the tenth anniversary of the *Challenger* space shuttle disaster, I watched an interview with June Scobee Rogers, Commander Dick Scobee's widow. She described her inspirational journey from being a victim of tragedy to being a survivor committed to carrying on the space mission.

She talked about how the affected families pulled together to create a legacy of the dream. She said they wanted to create "a living memorial that didn't dwell on how the crew died but on what they lived for." The families of the astronauts created the Challenger Center for promoting space science to children. During the past ten years, twenty-six centers have been built across the United States and Canada, and more than one million students have had the opportunity to experience the excitement of space and science through a simulated spaceflight.

As June Rogers described this process of founding the Challenger Center, she talked about turning the energies of grief and sadness into energies of creation and hope. She described the centers as "the way the mission continues," and said, "It reminds us that we should never quit reaching for the stars."

I was moved to tears as she concluded by saying, "I've touched the future—I teach." As I sat reflecting on her incredible courage and the faith she demonstrated by continuing to reach for the stars and turning tragedy into triumph, I thought about the unlimited power that we unleash when we ardently pursue our dreams. Through our dreams we create tomorrow.

Revitalize and Recreate a New Reality

The process of transformation begins with the recognition that change is required. Many change initiatives fail because managers and employees have not been convinced that change is necessary. Revitalization develops commitment and understanding to support change. It is a process of rekindling excitement for the future and establishing a mind-set for managing change.

Successful change processes capture the minds and hearts of an organization. Energy is mobilized and momentum is built when the following conditions occur:

- Change is recognized as a learning process. Team members understand that one change leads to another.

- Emphasis is placed on the "why" and "how" of change. Time is spent preparing for change by helping people understand the business context for the change.

- Long-term solutions are valued more than short-term quick fixes.

- Employees are involved and considered partners in the process. Involvement creates a shared understanding of the problem and affects the levels of commitment and learning.

Participation strengthens my commitment, because when I agree to be involved, it means I'm willing to be open to the possibility of something different. Participation demonstrates that at some level I have committed to a new way.

Simply involving employees, however, is not enough to overcome their resistance to change. Involvement must be at a meaningful level. Individuals must believe that they can contribute and that they have a part to play in making the change happen. Employees will only commit when they see that a change in responsibilities could actually make a difference.

An old Chinese proverb captures the essence of this process:
Tell me something and I may not remember.
Show me and I may not understand.
Involve me and I will remember.

Articulate a New Direction

The starting point for any effective change effort is a clearly defined new direction that acts as a reference point for day-to-day operations. To be transformative, the touchstone must be more than a goal. It must be a vision that people can rally around and use to prioritize activities or identify new opportunities. The vision must be easily understood, yet at the same time it must create a major shift in the corporate mind-set. Your vision statement must be broad enough to provide direction, yet flexible enough to implement in the real world.

The process of replacing old ways with new requires a strong sense of direction, a vision for the future and a level of persistence to break through the pain of altering the status quo. This commitment must be clearly shared and articulated if people are to embrace the change.

When he set out to transform General Electric, CEO Jack Welch focused on creating a plan of action that would significantly reshape GE's business. His philosophy was to make changes before he was forced to make them. His new direction was based on the question, "If we weren't already in the business, would we enter it today?" This defining question led to the development of the goal that every General Electric business must be either number one or number two in its market.

To achieve this goal, Welch took action to fix, close, or sell any division that didn't meet the standard. He established a three-phase action plan for achievement:

Step 1. Create a need for change. He laid off workers and sold businesses that couldn't be competitive.

Step 2. Create a future blueprint. He developed a strategy where individual businesses worked in isolation yet supported each other.

Step 3. Create new processes and practices to support the vision. He focused on innovation and productivity to ensure the future.

New Leadership for a New World

Effective leaders understand that transformation requires a different kind of leadership and that the role of managers must change. They understand that every situation is co-created and that in order for change to truly occur, there must be shared ownership and responsibility at all levels of the organization. They see leadership as a partnership and focus on creating an organization where power shifts from control and dependency to self-reliance and accessing internal energy.

When a true partnership between management and employees is formed, the relationship changes. A partnership changes the balance of power. It shifts the responsibility to joint accountability, which makes individuals at every level an integral part of the transformation. Each person helps to build the future by defining and carrying out the vision and implementing changes.

This new relationship requires a fundamental shift in how managers manage. It requires a conscious choice to shift the power by these means:

- Strengthening others through sharing information and involving them in decision-making.

- Fostering collaboration and building trust through sharing and openness.

- Increasing autonomy and allowing individuals to make decisions without looking over their shoulders or second-guessing.

- Creating strategic relationships to provide information, teach or mentor.

- Giving visibility to others and providing recognition for their efforts.

This redistribution of power opens the channel for more equal and honest sharing. Group discussions can now focus on asking questions, owning one's perceptions and feelings, and discussing conflicting needs. A partnership doesn't mean that both parties always get what they want, but it does mean everyone has a part to play and a voice to be heard.

Establishing a collaborative environment requires that we stop doing things the way they've always been done. We must undergo a significant shift in our mind-set about management's role. In *The Future Edge,* Joel Barker describes a paradigm as "a set of rules and regulations (written or unwritten) that tells you how to behave." He goes on to describe a paradigm shift as a "change to a new game, a new set of rules."

Creating this shift requires a willingness to undergo a transformation in our thinking and to re-examine the collective beliefs that block change. To effect this level of change in your organization, ask your group the following questions:

- What paradigms or beliefs are operating that limit our ability to achieve our goals?

- How do we perpetuate these limiting paradigms?

- Where does "us versus them" thinking create conflicts and limitations?

- What needs to change?

- What would support the desired mind-set shift?

- What one thing could I do differently today to produce the shift?

Strengthen through Self-Renewal

Organizational self-renewal is a cycle of continually reinforcing change by breaking down old patterns and building new ones. Self-renewal is an ongoing process of analyzing what's working well (and why), and then identifying what is not working and what needs to change. The process becomes self-perpetuating as old assumptions, beliefs, and patterns change, and new paradigms create new beliefs and new opportunities.

The key to establishing a self-renewing organization is to bring about a fundamental shift in the way people think, behave, and manage. We must change the way we understand the work we do and the relationships that affect our work. Each manager and employee must make conscious choices about the way they do their work.

We tend to resist changes that are thrust upon us, but we support ideas and changes that we help to create. One of the more effective and powerful ways to develop a renewal consciousness is by asking empowering open-ended questions.

Questions create automatic buy-in and commitment if they focus on supporting forward movement toward the objectives. For example, you could ask, "What are you pleased about accomplishing? What are you able to do better now than the past? What kind of support do you need to be successful?"

Empowering questions change our focus and help us to identify effective solutions. When I worked with Tony Robbins, I learned to ask a number of problem-solving questions:

- What's great about this? or, What could be great about this?

- What's not perfect yet?

- What am I willing to do to make it the way I want it?

- What am I no longer willing to do to have things the way I want?

- How can I do what is necessary to get this job done and enjoy the process?

Because each of these questions contains an assumption of a positive response, it changes the focus from an external perspective to unlocking the power within the individual. If we ask these questions on a consistent basis, we may discover that they can change our state of mind quickly and allow us to focus our energy on solutions rather problems.

Presuppositions can be incorporated into the structure of any question to create an empowering focus. Consider the following examples:

- Can you think of other applications for this information? (presupposes that the information can be applied)

- What can I learn from this? (presupposes there is something to learn)

- What would happen if you could find a solution? (presupposes a solution can be found)

- How do you know when you have done a good job? (presupposes the existence of an evaluative criteria for a job well done)

- How are all these situations alike? (presupposes that each situation is similar)

Effective questions liberate untapped potential by clarifying and changing the focus of our thinking and thereby shifting our energy. The intention behind the question determines its effectiveness. When we assume that people within our organization have solutions, we frame questions that demonstrate our interest and develop trust.

Close-ended questions that call for a "yes" or "no" answer discourage meaningful discussion, but open-ended questions create an opportunity to share thoughts and feelings. "Why" questions provoke resistance and defensiveness, whereas "what" or "how" questions encourage openness. Notice the difference between the following questions: "Is the program going well?" versus "What aspects of the program are going well?" The second question encourages more sharing of information and invites multiple responses.

Effective questions are an essential part of organizational renewal. They enable us to truly change by shifting our thoughts and paradigms, and they give us the power to discover new solutions to everyday issues.

Future Building through Today's Actions

Successful companies manage the future by using change to create a competitive advantage. These companies anticipate the future and use the trends of change—social, cultural, technological, economic, and lifestyle—to drive change within their organizations. They tap into company strengths and use day-to-day activities to build and create new directions.

To develop an environment and mind-set that supports change, utilize the following guidelines:

- Search for the hidden opportunity in a problem or trend and use each moment as a situation to become a student of change.

- Challenge assumptions and look for gaps in your information and your understanding of trends.

- Identify patterns that create threats or opportunities. To expand their business, McDonald's identified the demographic trend toward more single people and two-career couples who were purchasing fast food. They opened for breakfast and created a successful new product, the Egg McMuffin.

- Use breakthrough thinking to create new opportunities by changing the rules of the game. In 1973, Fred Smith was struggling to keep his aviation maintenance business alive because parts were arriving four or five days late. He saw a need for an overnight delivery service and created Federal Express, today a multibillion-dollar industry.

- Create innovative products or services in response to change by looking at the interconnection between change and what is needed. Shortly after the Canadian government announced the creation of a $2 coin, a university student designed and patented a special plastic mold to convert a section of a cash register to accommodate the coin. By the time the coin was released, the student had developed a million-dollar business.

Orchestrate Optimum Effectiveness

Transformation is affected by our thoughts and beliefs about change. Effective leaders understand that change occurs within a context or structure that shapes individual actions. They focus their attention on the *process* of change, not on the results of change. Because they view the organization as a system of interrelationships and patterns of connectedness, they understand that a change in one part affects and changes other parts. This web of connections is perceived as a large force field where elements are constantly acting upon and reacting to each other, creating transactional patterns.

This systemic view creates a new way to look at change. It shifts the focus from a reactive cause-and-effect relationship to the broader context that created the conditions for the reaction. It sees a problem as embedded in or surrounded by a force field that keeps it intact and operating in the system. Lasting change will only occur if we alter the structure within which we operate.

If a solution only deals with an immediate problem without addressing its fundamental cause, a problem might be solved in the short term but will recycle itself into a more critical issue. Thus, for lasting change to occur, there must be a shift in the surrounding force field or underlying structure.

Successful organizations use a systemic mind-set to create high leverage points of change by observing recurring patterns of behavior and intervening at the underlying or root cause. By moving to a systemic view, it is possible to see how today's problems were created by previous choices, decisions and behaviors. This balcony viewpoint creates an opportunity to determine the best point of intervention that can modify the underlying context and produce a lasting change.

At the individual level, we can move from a reactive perspective to a systemic view by asking the question, "What would I have to believe in order to feel this way?" By changing the structure of the situation, we allow ourselves to change our state of consciousness and choose a different belief, thereby shifting the direction of our personal energy. Or if we're looking at our involvement in a situation, we can move to a higher systemic view by shifting our attention and asking, "What am I doing to invite this response?"

Intervention and shift of team or organizational patterns occurs by blocking some transactions, encouraging others, or repositioning and lessening the impact of certain behaviors. For example, if we're working with a team that seems to be struggling with direction, we could focus on the interactions and boundaries between the supervisor and the rest of the team. We could look for ways in which confusion occurs, such as unclear boundaries (the supervisor interfering in a subordinate's work) or a complementarity relationship (lack of supervisor direction resulting in few subordinate requests for guidance). We could then intervene to shift the pattern by encouraging and coaching the supervisor.

Revolutionary Cultural Change

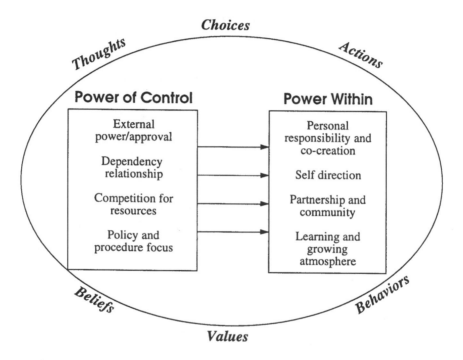

Unleashing your corporate knowledge requires a revolutionary shift of the organization's culture. It requires new ways of thinking, being, and doing—a radical shift from the power of external control to the power inside the organization and within individuals by examining traditions, setting new precedents, and establishing supportive practices. Changing the corporate culture creates an atmosphere of personal responsibility and self-direction and a establishes a partnership of learning and growing between the organization and the individual.

The steps necessary to shift the culture can be applied at all three levels— individual, team, and organization. This activity is a three-step process of identifying the thoughts, choices, and actions necessary to make the change. For each environmental characteristic, ask the following questions:

- What would we have to believe? (thoughts)
- What would we value? (choices)
- What behaviors would be required? (actions)

The following chart is an example of this process:

THOUGHTS	CHOICES	ACTIONS
What would we have to believe?	*What would we value?*	*What behaviors would be required?*
Personal responsibility and co-creation • Authority comes from within • We own our own actions • Everyone's contribution is vital	• Self expression • Each contribution • Openness and sharing	• Leadership's role to focus on vision • Less structure – more flexible boundaries • Direct and authentic interaction
Self direction • Empowerment is a state of mind • A vision or passion exists within each of us • We engage in activities that have significant meaning for us	• Initiative and risk-taking • Test our own assumptions • Courage to say no	• Supervisor's task is to help people trust their instincts and to take responsibility for success • Ask people to choose, express needs directly and to make commitments • Confront our own attitudes about maintaining control
Partnership and Community • Self interest is interdependent with others and the interest of the business • Everyone contributes	• Co-operation and teamwork • Individual strengths and contribution	• Success of organization is primary reward system • Act as partners with customers – committed to customer's success • Eliminate departments or functions created simply to control
Learning and growing atmosphere • We are the architect of the future • Change occurs through the choices and decisions we make • Learning and growing is part of choice making	• Freedom to try, fail and learn • Creating new rules and a new way	• Give others ownership and freedom to choose path / direction • Maintain integrity by walking our talk • Consistency between plans and actions

Maintain Momentum

Successful companies learn to build and maintain momentum so that each step of the transformation is used to move toward their goals. Momentum is established according to the following guidelines:

- Understand, teach, and reinforce that the current reality is always changing, so it can easily be realigned and molded to create new results.

- Assimilate lessons learned and insights gained into future steps by experimenting. Use emerging challenges and accumulated experience to inform and power new decisions.

- Use each decision as a method to gain a broader perspective and to anticipate future developments.

- Apply accumulated knowledge and wisdom to unique situations and thereby invent new steps and methods.

- Capitalize on successes to create enthusiasm and involve others in participation.

- Use strategic moments to consciously choose a new direction and redefine the results that support moving forward. The key is to recognize the current reality for what it is and use it to redirect our efforts.

Create momentum by allowing one idea to lead to another and another like ripples expanding from a pebble tossed into a lake. Tap into the group's collective consciousness by creating opportunities for collaboration within and between groups. Create a formal process to learn from each other and to identify, test, and evaluate ideas. Include the following steps:

1. Identify and share insights.
2. Clarify interpretations and assumptions.
3. Decide how this information impacts the group.
4. State issues or concerns.
5. Decide on a course of action.

Discover underused assets and explore new options by taking advantage of your strengths. Examine your business and processes for any assets you could employ differently right now. Be inquisitive and question why things are the way they are. Look at what is special about your company and find out how it is different from competitors. Ask: How could these strengths be better utilized? Are there other ways to use our customer base, prospect lists, and distribution channels to increase our business? What are other companies doing successfully that we could cmulate and apply differently within our business? What are useful benchmarks, and who has the best practices? What can we learn from others, and how can we leverage the lessons we learn?

It is not because things are difficult
that we do not dare,
it is because we do not dare
that they are difficult.

—Seneca

Even if you're on the right track, you'll get run over if you just sit there.

—Will Rogers

The best way to predict the future is to create it.

—Peter Drucker

Chapter 15

Control Your Destiny

The essence and purpose of unleashing our internal power is to enable any individual, organization, or team to take control of its destiny. Facing new challenges, seizing new opportunities, choosing to change, climbing to new heights, and reaching for the stars and beyond consists of the following steps:

Don Casson

Directional Adjustment

When a boat sets sail, the crew constantly make adjustments to maintain course and arrive at the desired destination. They navigate by shifting speed and direction to take advantage of the wind and sea conditions. Similarly, an organization navigating the unknown waters of transformation must set sail with a clear destination in mind but be willing to shift speed and direction to take advantage of market conditions and to weather the competitive storms.

In *Corporate Transformation,* Ralph Kilmann categorizes these shifts and changes into four groups:

Tuning: incremental changes made in anticipation of future events (for example, decrease costs through increased productivity).

Adaptation: incremental changes made in reaction to external events (for example, responding to competition).

Reorientation: strategic change created from anticipated external events (such as the effects of globalization).

Re-creation: strategic changes necessitated by life-threatening external events (such as a merger of competitors that allows them to control the market).

Controlling your own destiny is achieved through the process of reorientation—that is, strategic change created by consciously choosing to adjust your direction rather than reacting to conditions. Reorientation assumes an anticipatory mind-set and attitude that focuses on creating opportunities to move forward.

For example, when Jack Welch identified the goal that General Electric should be either number one or number two in a market, his measuring stick was position of market share in the United States. By the mid-1980s, Welch anticipated that leadership in the domestic market would no longer ensure success or survivability in an environment of globalization, and he shifted GE's focus to its world market positions.

As a result of this shift, the game, the rules, and whom GE viewed as its competitors all changed. Instead of competing solely against other U.S. companies like Westinghouse, GE was now pitted against companies like Siemens of Germany and Toshiba of Japan. To compete against these companies, GE reoriented its operating model. Jack Welch shifted the focus of each business within GE to take responsibility for its own globalization. He developed a concept of ownership under which managers were able to operate their businesses as if they owned them. Welch focused on creating an atmosphere where employees would take responsibility for making the required changes.

Engage and Expand Environment

Perhaps paradoxically, controlling your own destiny requires a partnership with others or a willingness to work together to create environmental conditions that ensure mutual success and durability. Partnerships in the following four areas enable an organization to significantly influence and control its environmental conditions.

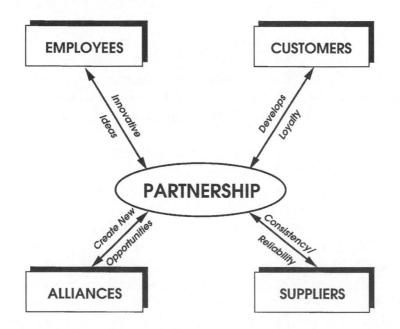

Employees

When a true partnership culture is created internally, all external interactions—with customers, suppliers and competitors—are changed. The partnership paradigm establishes a new way of perceiving, thinking, and valuing associations. It establishes a climate of open interaction by encouraging a willingness to listen and to share ideas and information. Increased communication creates acceptance and trust, which cycles back and opens the gates of interaction further.

As communication, acceptance, and trust grow, individual contributions increasingly are treated with respect, which ignites interactive problem-solving and creativity and fosters breakthrough thinking. Breakthrough thinking uncovers more options to solve problems and creates new opportunities. New opportunities open the horizons to increased vision and corporate energy, which in turn creates a new level of optimism and excitement that powers ongoing change. What seemed impossible before now seems probable. What once required permission now fuels consensus.

When genuine partnerships are encouraged, employee relationships shift from separate and competitive to supportive, interactive and mutually benefi- cial. Frank Stronoch built a billion-dollar company by making his managers rich. His management philosophy has been to "get the best people and give them a piece of the action." This philosophy started early in his career when, as a young Austrian toolmaker, he immigrated to Canada and went into business for himself. He built a small business of twenty people and had just landed a contract with General Motors when his foreman wanted to leave to set up his own business. Stronoch offered the foreman the opportunity to open up a new factory and own part of it. He offered him a base salary and one-third of the profits.

The idea worked so successfully that today Stronoch has eighty-seven factories in his company, Magria International Inc., which has become one of the world's largest auto-parts manufacturers, with annual sales of over $2.5 billion. He builds each operation on the concept of empowering the foreman to run the business as an independent profit center. Many of his managers make up to $500,000 a year with a successful operation (typically a manager is paid $60,000 base and 3 to 5 percent of the factory's gross profit). When he took the company public, he gave employees shares entitling them to 10 percent of the total profits.

Affiliated teams can learn from each other's experience and profit from each other's success. Cooperative relationships decrease the intensity and level of risk-taking by establishing tolerance for experimentation, failure and learning.

Customers

Establishing partnerships with your customers allows you to leverage the creative energy within other companies and build a competitive advantage by tailoring your products and services to meet true needs. This requires focusing on the lifetime value of the customer and shifting the collective consciousness from "selling what we make" to "making what our customers need." Today's successful companies make it a point to know and cater to their customers' changing needs. For example, the Four Seasons Hotel chain understands the importance of adding value to their customers. They recognized that their customers were constantly dealing with pressures of jet lag, stress, and time constraints and that they needed to provide service that eliminated hassles and fatigue. This led to the introduction of the concierge service—a service specially designed to support the customer that has now become the standard for all top-end hotels.

Customer partnerships take the guesswork out of the value-added equation by establishing an effective process whereby the customers can communicate their needs. Developing customer value doesn't necessarily mean expensive product research and development. In fact, it can be a very simple and fun process. Tim Boyle, CEO of Columbia Sportswear Company, has created a unique formula for product development. He invites customers from across the country to accompany him on fishing and hunting trips. He supplies participants with Columbia Sportswear gear and returns from each trip with new product ideas or modification to existing ones. After one such trip he changed the pocket on a fishing vest. On another he noticed the group shivering from the cold wind blowing on their necks; by taking off a detachable collar from another coat, he quickly improvised and created a new feature for the hunting jacket.

The key to product development is your interaction with the customer. Boyle sums up his process this way: "We want a simple method to create a product. We talk to the customer. Then we make it. Then they buy it."

Partnering with a customer shifts the energy in both organizations toward togetherness and support—working to create innovative and mutually beneficial solutions. Effective partnerships are built on the following foundations:

- Understand your customers' processes and current needs. Look at how your customers use your products or services, and examine present problems.

- Assist your customers to understand future needs and match product capabilities to both current and anticipated requirements.

- Create innovative customer solutions that match future customer needs to new product development or quality enhancement.

These steps are easy to implement and can produce significant results. One of my former clients, a large manufacturing company, found that when they focused on understanding one of their customer's processes and how the flow valve they manufactured fit into that process, they were able to make significant improvements to the product and decrease product returns by approximately 40 percent. These enhancements not only impacted the company's bottom line significantly, but the change in customer relations led to the development of new products that expanded the company's business.

Suppliers

Partnering with suppliers works the same way as customer alliances. Every company has an urgent need to reduce costly inventories as well as to improve its own delivery times and product quality. Partnering with suppliers can help to identify ways of decreasing waste, lost time, and errors in production. Working closely with your suppliers to make sure they understand your process, standards, and special needs enhances their ability to match your standards so that you can meet your customers' requirements.

Effective supplier partnerships are built on trust and involvement over time. Establishing trust requires more than just words. It requires a shift from an adversarial, competitive bidding system to developing long-term relationships where multi-year contracts are assured if standards are met.

In the mid-1980s, Xerox pioneered a change in supplier relationships. They reduced the number of parts suppliers they used from five thousand to four hundred and developed an education program for these preferred suppliers. Xerox established a top management interface committee to meet with suppliers to discuss Xerox's needs and the suppliers' concerns. They introduced a supplier improvement program aimed at helping suppliers make changes to their products They invited suppliers to visit Xerox plants and sponsored trips to Japan where their suppliers could see required changes firsthand.

Over time, as the supplier partnership developed, Xerox was able to eliminate waste and paperwork by establishing an electronic network of suppliers, which ultimately resulted in shorter delivery times and better, more consistent deliveries. Xerox was able to pool the resources of different suppliers and decrease the cost of manufacturing materials, thereby creating a win-win situation: suppliers were assured of long-term contracts, and Xerox's cost of production decreased.

Alliances

Joining forces in mutually beneficial alliances opens new markets and creates new opportunities for products and services. Strategic alliances allow a firm's competitive advantage to be strengthened in the following ways:

- Increased core business concentration—An alliance of unrelated business units can increase each unit's concentration in its core business.

- Horizontal integration—An alliance between two firms with competing or overlapping businesses can strengthen both. For example, the alliance between Canadian Airlines and American Airlines in effect added key routes to both carriers.

- Vertical integration—Alliances with sources of supply or major customers may lower costs and increase the value added to the product. For example, Pepsi-Cola's alliance with an independent bottlers association lowered Pepsi's cost of distribution while opening new markets for the bottlers.

- Diversification into an unrelated business—An alliance between two previously unrelated industries may open opportunities for both businesses. For example, some food retailers and financial services companies have linked up and opened mini-branches of the financial company, resulting in increased convenience for customers of both organizations.

An effective alliance is created through a willingness to search out opportunities to work together and to explore complementary relationships. Successful alliances require a period of getting to know each other's strengths and weaknesses and time to build a foundation of trust, open communication, and collaboration.

Each organization must appraise prospective relationships and determine compatibility by using these strategies:

- Examining how the firm's competitive advantage will be embraced or changed.

- Clarifying and testing all assumptions and identifying requirements for change.

- Determining potential impacts on employees and shareholders.

- Identifying management's commitment of time and resources.

- Planning how best to communicate the decision, with the understanding that every action and word send a message about the future.

- Creating an implementation plan to ensure that sufficient resources are available to optimize the transition.

Strength through Strategies

Many delayering and downsizing initiatives have not been successful because the only difference has been that fewer people are doing the work— the work itself has not changed. To remain competitive through changing environmental conditions, organizations must evolve and create fundamentally different patterns of strategies, systems, and structures. To redesign a business, the work itself must be redefined.

In 1988, General Electric introduced a program called "workout" to eliminate unnecessary work and increase employee participation and involvement. The concept was to eliminate bureaucratic red tape by allowing frontline employees to solve problems.

Groups of thirty to one hundred employees spent three days off-site discussing key problems and developing specific solution proposals. On the final day of the session, managers reviewed the proposals and made immediate decisions on the suggestions.

Over the next few years, the workout processes evolved to include cross-functional teams working together to solve specifically defined problems. Business processes were mapped out and examined for value-added steps, and changes were made to the processes to eliminate unnecessary work. Cycle times were enhanced, incentives were developed, and problem areas were dealt with.

Sometimes when organizations redefine their business, organizational structure becomes the focal point and driving force for change. Members push to redraw the organization chart and get back to business as usual, instead of revising processes to optimize operations. What is forgotten is that form must follow function—structure comes out of process, not the other way around.

As processes are redefined, structural issues become evident. Leaders within the organization must exercise courage to adapt the corporate structure to fit the emerging processes.

If structure is to effectively contribute to the company's competitive advantage, it must be linked to the process and the core competencies necessary to produce the desired outcome. In *Rethinking the Corporation,* Robert Tomasko says that "corporate superstructures must be rethought so they reflect the new reality that power needs to be expressed via knowledge and experience."

The easiest way to develop this core competency linkage is to incorporate it as part of the restructuring process. For example, when I assisted a large telecommunications company a few years ago, we identified key strategic positions that would be instrumental in driving the new direction. For each of these positions, we identified key criteria for the breadth and depth of experience necessary to provide the background for effective decision-making.

These criteria were then used as benchmarks for the succession planning system and for creating development plans for managers. The advancement paths were related to key business issues or strategic changes. Experience in certain product lines or divisions became a prerequisite for movement into the position, which not only aligned skills to the new strategic direction but also set the context for changing of the old guard.

Translate into Action

Controlling your corporate destiny is about taking action to direct the changes in your organization and to incorporate these changes into daily operational activities.

Initiating transformation is a five-step process that overcomes resistance to change and builds expertise to manage future changes. Each step lays the foundation for the next by reinforcing the importance of the change and building commitment and momentum.

Step 1. Make sure that everyone understands the proposed change and why it is necessary. Even in organizations with highly participative decision-making processes, whenever changes are implemented, every individual in the organization naturally wonders, "What does this change mean for me?" Organizations that successfully navigate transformation take advantage of both planned and unplanned opportunities to develop shared expectations and continually reinforce the need to change. Creating a climate for ongoing change is not a "once and for all" accomplishment. The importance of continual change and improvement must be woven into the fabric of the organization and underscored at every opportunity through meetings, discussions about vision, and tangible symbols of the new direction.

Step 2. Reduce resistance by acknowledging the underlying fears and concerns of the individuals affected by the change. Clarify anticipated results of the change and openly discuss specific questions regarding security issues such as "Will I have a job?" or "What will I need to give up in order for this change to occur?"

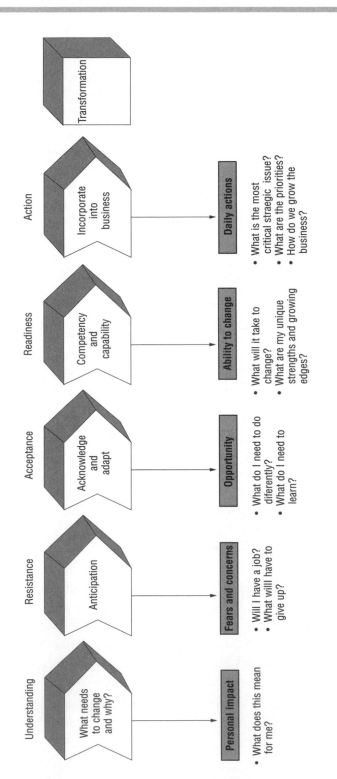

Step 3. Create acceptance by helping individuals see the opportunity and benefits of the change. Make it clear what will need to be done differently and what will need to be learned. Develop plans to assist and support individuals through the transition.

Step 4. Develop readiness for change by developing resources to help team members grow and expand their capabilities. When people accept the idea of change, they are open to exploring ways to gain the new required competencies. The organization must support and encourage readiness before individuals can be expected to embrace change.

Step 5. Take action to minimize disruption by incorporating daily actions into ongoing business processes. Focus attention on the most critical strategic issues and identify key priorities that will support the growth of the business.

Integration and Improvement Process

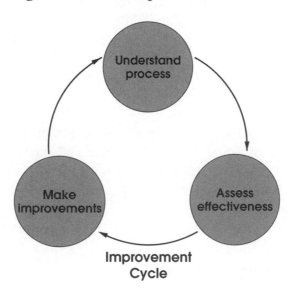

To redesign its business and effectively adapt to changing environmental conditions, an organization must clearly understand and control its daily work processes. A process is any activity or group of activities that takes an input, transforms it, and provides an output to an internal or external customer. Process improvement is a three-phase cycle that seeks to increase productivity and improve customer satisfaction by simplifying processes and eliminating non-value-added complexity.

All processes are intended to transform inputs into outputs that meet customer needs, but unless they evolve to accommodate changing requirements and shifts in technology, processes may retain steps that no longer contribute directly to the value of the output. Any worthwhile improvement cycle must incorporate three important phases in order to bring about the necessary and desired changes and improvements.

Phase 1: Understand the process. Develop a clear picture of how the current process operates. Define the process in terms of its boundaries (beginning and end points) and its interfaces (suppliers, customers, inputs and outputs). Document the process workflow at a high level, clarify customer requirements, and determine specific key process decision points where action taken will result in conformance to customer requirements.

A flow chart is a useful tool for diagramming all major process steps. This sequential pictorial representation of the inputs, activities, decision points, and outputs can then be analyzed to provide insight into value-added activities and inefficiencies. Flow charts identify and illustrate problems by demonstrating how different steps in the process relate to each other. The purpose of a flow chart is to accurately identify the work process as it is presently done. The diagram on page 162 is an example of a process flow chart.

Phase 2: Assess effectiveness. Focus on creating reliable processes that will ensure that your customers receive exactly what they need when they want it. Evaluate all key processes for performance and measure each against a control standard. This phase is the starting point of improvement because it provides the baseline data that establishes the foundation for incremental or breakthrough changes.

To assess the effectiveness of a process, analyze the flow chart and identify key process points by asking the following questions:

- Does this activity add value?
- Is it needed?
- What are obvious redundancies?
- Should someone else perform the work activity?
- Should activities be combined?
- Should activities be run in parallel instead of series?

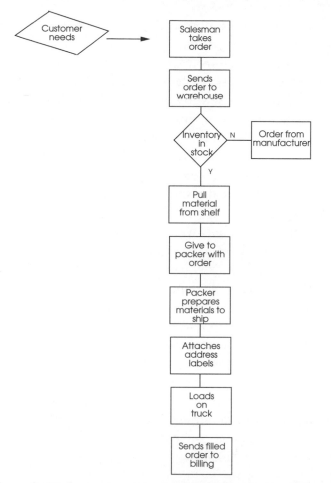

Phase 3: Make improvements. Use this step to change the current process by restructuring, shortening, simplifying, or strengthening the overall activity. At this stage, you can make corrections to obvious problems such as redundancies, gaps, and unneeded tasks. Add control points and measurements to track performance and identify other process improvement areas.

Next Generation of Products/Services

In today's rapidly changing business climate, customer service is more important than ever. Distinctive service can be the best way to develop and sustain customer loyalty and establish a competitive advantage. Despite all the talk about meeting customer needs, many companies still do not understand the true meaning of customer service. These companies often send mixed messages to their customers.

I was recently in a large chain store that emphasizes its commitment to friendly, helpful service by stationing an employee at the door to greet incoming customers. Although the greeter establishes a positive initial impression, unless the customer experiences friendly, helpful, convenient service throughout the store, the retailer has failed to establish truly distinctive customer service. In my case, I was buying a number of items and took them to a cashier. She attempted to ring up the purchase, but the cash register rejected the sale price and would only accept the regular price. The clerk had to add and delete items five or six times before the transaction was completed. I paid for the items, but when I received the receipt I noticed that I had been charged for three items that should have been deleted. When I requested a refund, I was told I would need to stand in another line (with six other people waiting) to receive a refund. When I inquired about another way to expedite the process, the manager told me that their procedure was the only way. As you can imagine, I didn't walk away from the transaction feeling like a valued customer.

At the other end of the customer-service spectrum is the experience I had at Nordstrom, a department store chain based in Seattle that truly understands how to care for its customers. Nordstrom gives its salespeople the freedom to shop with the customer, putting together a wardrobe with items from different departments within the store. With friendly, courteous employees who know the store's products and can match merchandise to the customer's needs, Nordstrom has created a positive shopping experience that brings customers back time and again. This personal touch is part of a distinct competitive advantage that Nordstrom has established.

Yes to Change

Every change and every new situation are opportunities to control your own destiny. Change means growth, learning, and new opportunities that only become possible with a shift in perception, thinking, beliefs or behaviors. Change creates more change. Once we have established movement by initiating change, we gain the advantage of momentum. We can then use the power of change to our advantage to grow and expand in new ways. Momentum allows us to build success one step at a time without having to start from scratch each time.

Each change is a choice to focus on what we want to create and take steps to control our destiny. Continuous change becomes a series of celebrations as we mark our successful outcomes and herald new beginnings. In the midst of change, we preserve stability by continually clarifying the reasons for change, and we constantly build trust by listening to our teammates' concerns and implementing their ideas. Look for ways to help employees through the pain and adjustments that are a natural part of the growth process, and don't forget to celebrate accomplishments along the way. Over time, continuity replaces old definitions of stability as the organization builds on its strengths and consistently applies the lessons it has learned.

Take Action Now

The time to begin is now, and the place to begin is with yourself. Even if you lack hierarchical power within your organization, by tapping into the power within yourself you can influence and educate those around you to begin to unleash their own personal energy. Pick a starting point and begin to unlock the power within yourself and within your organization.

Bring your vision to life by living it at each step. Take action based on your values and vision and let them direct and guide your decisions. Use your intuition as a compass to guide you in the direction of your dreams.

Plan small wins and celebrate incremental progress. Create a readiness for change by taking one step at a time and let the power of momentum carry you to the next level. Experiment and learn from your successes *and* your failures.

Create choice. Help others to understand that we all have alternatives and acknowledge progress by celebrating each step.

Make choices visible. When choices and actions are publicly displayed, momentum is created that kick-starts further change. For example, a large manufacturing company, focusing on zero defects, had each of its 6,000-plus employees commit to the goal by signing posters mounted on the walls throughout the corporation. At the individual level, post your vision statement and values in your work area, both as a reminder to yourself and as a statement to others of the guiding forces in your life.

See the process as an adventure. Don't be discouraged by occasional setbacks and struggles along the way. Each step and each mistake provide insight and experience that sets the foundation for the next step. Have fun creating the organization you want. Remember, large-scale change occurs when a lot of people change just a little.

The time to move ahead
is just before you think you are ready.

—Robert Fritz

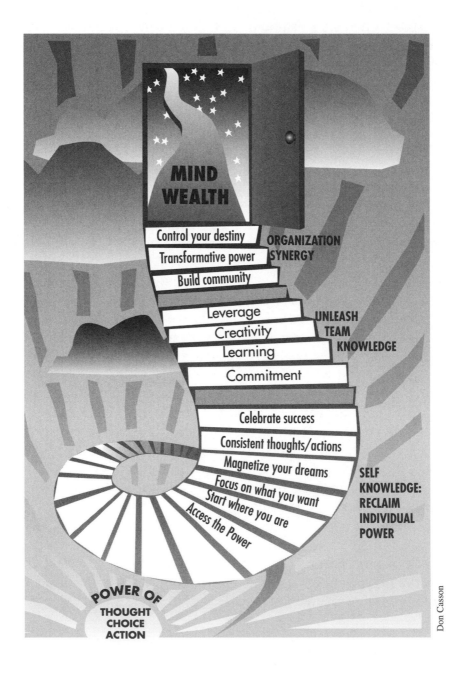

Don Casson

Bibliography

Agor, W. H. *Intuitive Management: Integrating left and right brain management skills*. New York, NY: Prentice-Hall, 1984.

Albrecht, K. and R. Zemke. *Service in America: Doing business in the new economy*. Homewood, IL: Dow Jones-Irwin, 1985.

Allen, J. *As a Man Thinketh*. Santa Fe, NM: Sun Books, 1983.

Barker, J. *Future Edge: Discovering the new paradigms of success*. New York, NY: William Morrow, 1992.

Block, P. *The Empowered Manager: Positive political skills at work*. San Francisco, CA: Jossey-Bass, 1987.

Buzan, T. *The Mind Map Book: Radiant thinking the major evolution in human thought*. London: BBC Enterprises Ltd, 1993.

Capra, F. *The Turning Point: Science, society and the rising culture*. New York, NY: Bantam, 1982.

Carlzon, J. *Moments of Truth: New strategies for today's customer driven economy*. New York, NY: Harper and Row, 1987.

Cole-Whittaker, T. *How to Have More in a Have Not World*. New York, NY: Rawson Associates, 1983.

Covey, S. *The Seven Habits of Highly Effective People,* New York, NY: Simon and Schuster, 1989.

DeBono, E. *Lateral Thinking: Creativity step by step*. New York, NY: Harper and Row, 1990.

— —. *Opportunities*. Middlesex, England: Penguin, 1980.

Dyer, W. *Real Magic: Creating miracles in everyday life*. New York, NY: Harper Collins, 1992.

Fezler, W. *Creative Imagery: How to visualize in all five senses*. New York, NY: Fireside–Simon and Schuster, 1989.

Friedman, N. *Bridging Science and Spirit: Common elements in David Bohm's physics*. St. Louis, MO: Living Lake Books, 1990.

Fritz, R. *Creating*. New York, NY: Ballantine, 1991.

— —. *The Path of Least Resistance*. Hanover, MA: Stillpoint, 1984.

Gawain, S. *Creative Visualization*. San Rafael, CA: New World Library, 1978.

Hill, N. *Think and Grow Rich*. New York, NY: Ballantine, 1960.

Heider, J. *The Tao of Leadership*. New York, NY: Bantam, 1985.

Jacobson, G. and J. Hillkirk. *Xerox American Samurai*. New York, NY: Macmillan, 1986.

Jampolsky, G. *Love is Letting Go of Fear*. Berkeley, CA: Celestial Arts, 1999.

Johnson, S. *The Precious Present*. Garden City, NY: Doubleday, 1984.

Kanter. R. M. *When Giants Learn to Dance*. New York, NY: Simon and Schuster, 1989.

Keyes, K. *Handbook to Higher Consciousness*. Coos Bay, OR: Love Line Books, 1995.

Kilmann, R. and T. J. Covin. *Corporate Transformation: Revitalizing organizations for a competitive world*. San Francisco, CA: Jossey-Bass, 1988.

Kline, P. and B. Saunders. *Ten Steps to a Learning Organization*. Arlington, VA: Great Ocean, 1993.

Kouzes, J. and B. Posner. *The Leadership Challenge: How to get extraordinary things done in organizations*. San Francisco, CA: Jossey-Bass, 1987.

McNeil, A. *The I of the Hurricane*. Toronto: Stoddart, 1987.

Miller, W. *The Creative Edge: Fostering innovation where you work*. Reading, MA: Addison-Wesley, 1986.

Mizuno, S. *Management for Quality Improvement: The seven new QC tools*. Cambridge, MA: Productivity Press, 1988.

Murphy, J. *The Power of Your Subconscious Mind*. Engelwood Cliffs, NJ: Prentice-Hall. 1963.

Naisbitt, J. *Global Paradox*. New York, NY: Avon, 1995.

Noe, J. *Peak Performance Principles for High Achievers*. New York, NY: Berkley, 1984.

Oakley, E. and D. Krug. *Enlightened Leadership: Getting to the heart of change*. New York, NY: Simon and Schuster, 1991.

Pater, R. *Martial Arts and the Art of Management: Strategies for creativity, power and control*. Rochester, VT: Destiny Books, 1988.

Peck, S. *The Different Drum: Community making and peace*. New York, NY: Touchstone, 1987.

Peters. T. *Thriving on Chaos: Handbook for a management revolution*. New York, NY: Alfred A. Knopf, 1987.

Porter, M. *Competitive Advantage: Creating and sustaining superior performance*. New York, NY: Collier Macmillan, 1985.

Riley, P. *The Winner Within: A life plan for team players*. New York, NY: Putnam, 1993.

Robbins, A. *Awaken the Giant Within*. New York, NY: Summit/Simon and Schuster, 1991.

Rodgers, J. S. *Silver Linings: Triumph of the Challenger 7*. Macon, GA: Smyth and Helwys, 1996.

Schuller, R. *Tough Times Never Last, But Tough People Do*. New York, NY: Bantam, 1983.

Senge, P. *The Fifth Discipline: The art and practice of the learning organization*. New York, NY: Doubleday, 1990.

Stewart, T. *Intellectual Capital: The new wealth of organizations*. New York, NY: Doubleday/Currency, 1997.

Talbot, M. *The Holographic Universe*. New York, NY: Harper Collins, 1991.

Tichy, N. and S. Sherman. *Control Your Destiny or Someone Else Will*. New York, NY: Doubleday/Currency, 1993.

Toffler, A. Powershift: *Knowledge, wealth and violence at the edge of the 21st century*. New York, NY: Bantam, 1990.

Tomasko, R. *Rethinking the Corporation: The Architecture of change*. New York, NY: American Management Association, 1993.

Waitley, D. *Seeds of Greatness*. New York, NY: Ballantine, 1985.

Wheatley, M. *Leadership and the New Science: Learning about organization from an orderly universe*. San Francisco, CA: Barrett-Koehler, 1992.

Viscott, D. *Risking*. New York, NY: Pocket Books, 1977.

Zukav, G. *Seat of the Soul*. New York, NY: Fireside/Simon and Schuster, 1989.

About The Author

Janet Slemko is an internationally recognized leader in the field of change implementation. She is president of IMTC and a senior partner with MindWealth Inc. She has more than twenty-seven years of experience in strategic planning, executive and management development, organizational effectiveness and operations management. She has a master's degree in applied behavioral science and has consulted in both the public and private sectors in a variety of industries.

Janet has provided consulting services to corporate and divisional line management in strategic planning, team building, values clarification, TQM, learning organizations and knowledge management. She has worked with numerous Fortune 500 companies across North America, including Alberta Power, Baxter Corporation, BellCore Research, BellSouth, Human Resources Development Canada, Galxo, PanCanadian Petroleum, Northern Telecom, Northrop Corporation and Telus Corporation

For information regarding lectures, workshops, and consulting contact:

In USA:
MindWealth Inc.
Phone (206) 366-2180
Fax (206) 545-7207
E-mail: jslemko@mindwealth.com

In Canada:
IMTC
Phone (403) 249-5613
Fax (403) 686-4020

MindWealth Inc.

     MindWealth Inc. is an international company that is dedicated to facilitating the awareness, understanding and implementation of intellectual capital. Our strategic intent is to be a world leader in the adaptation of a new mind set for organizing and operating corporations and businesses.

     Our goal is to create an environment that brings about the best of individuals and organizations by accessing the power within. MindWealth Inc. offers the following products and customized services for the identification, management and leveraging of untapped assets of an organization:

- Strategies and tools to leverage and capitalize on knowledge.

- Examples of best practices to convert intellectual capital into competitive advantages.

- Facilitating emerging information and resources for specific applications to implement practical business solutions.

- Experiential activities to explore ways to activate individual and team potential.

     For additional information regarding all the services available through MindWealth Inc. contact:

MindWealth Inc.
4505 University Way N.E.
Suite 383
Seattle, Washington 98105

Phone: 206-366-2180
Fax: 206-545-7207
E-mail: jslemko@mindwealth.com

To order additional copies of

MindWealth™

Book U.S.: $15.95   Shipping/Handling: $3.50
Book Canada: $23.95   Shipping/Handling: Actual Cost

Contact: **BookPartners, Inc.**
P.O. Box 922
Wilsonville, OR 97070

E-mail: bpbooks@teleport.com
Fax: 503-682-8684
Phone: 503-682-9821
Order: 1-800-895-7323